TOWARDS UNDERSTANDING MANAGEMENT PRINCIPLES AND PROCESS

Towards Understanding Management Principles and Process

Copyright©: 2011-2018
Dr. W. A. Khan
ISBN: 9781791677060

CAUTION: The readers are requested to respect this book as it contains orginal text of the Quran!

Published by:

Dr. W. A. Khan
Uxbridge, London
First Edition – 2018
ISBN: 9781791677060

Dr Wazir Ali Khan

BOOKS IN SEARCH OF MANAGEMENT EXCELLENCE SERIES

Table of Contents

7.1   INTODUCTION
7.2   WHAT IS SCIENTIFIC MANAGEMENT?
7.3   SCIENTIFIC MANAGEMENT BY TAYLOR
7.4   FAYOL VS. TAYLOR ON THE STUDY OF SCIENTIFIC MANAGEMENT
7.5   PRINCIPLES OF SCIENTIFIC MANAGEMENT
7.6   TOOLS AND TECHNIQUES OF SCIENTIFIC MANAGEMENT
7.6.1   Time Study
7.6.2   Motion Study
7.6.3   Differential Piece Wage Plan
7.6.4   Functional Foremanship
7.6.5   Standardization
7.6.4   Other Tools and Techniques
7.7   CRITICISM OF SCIENTIFIC MANAGEMENT

8.1   INTRODUUCTION
8.2   PLANNING FUNCTION OF MANAGEMENT
8.3   ORGANIZING FUNCTION OF MANAGEMENT
8.4   STAFFING FUNCTION OF MANAGEMENY
8.5   LEADING/DIRECTING FUNCTION OF MANAGEMENT
8.6   CONTROLLING FUNCTION OF MANAGEMENT

FOREWORD

The specific purpose of the "In Search of Management series" is to provide comprensive knowledge, skills, and know-how to students perusing their studies, in general and fields of management/administration and allied subjects in particular. The series in its totality will provide guideline to all managers at all level from foreman to chief executive engaged in all industries, trade and commerce

This book in No.1 in the series and is aiming at providing the awareness to all members of the market economy in general and to potential managers in particulars. This book is No. 1 in the series and consists of 13 chapters. Chapter 1 consists of introduction. Chapter 2 consists of 'management and manager defined' and includes: what is management which frther includes: General Defnitio; Management as a Process; Management as an Activity; Management as a Discipline; Management as a Discipline; Management as a Group; Management as both Science and Art; Management as a Profession. It includes manager defined.

Chapter 3 consists of Principles of Management and includes: introduction; Hanri Fayol's principles of management; features of principles of management; and importance of the principles of management. Chapter 4 consists of levels and areas of management and includes: introduction; principal objectives of management; levels of management (including top level management, middle level management and lower level management); and areas of management. Chapter 5 consists of importance and significance of management. Chapter 6 consists of asministration vs. Managements.

Chapter 7 consists of 'scientific management in theory and practice' and includes: introduction; what is scientific management; scientific management by taylor; Fayol vs. Taylor on the study of scientific management; principles of scientific management; tools and techniques of scientific management, which further includes: time study, motion study, differential piece wage plan, functional foremanship, standardization, and other tools and techniques; and criticism of scientific management. Chapter 8 consists of 'the management process: the fuctions of management and includes: introduction; planning function of management; organizing function of management; staffing function of managemeny; leading/directing function of management; and controlling function of management.

Chapter 9 consists of management theories briefly explained. Chapter 10 consists of roles and skills of managers. Chapter 11 consists of the nature of organizational environment. Chapter 12 consists of Islamic perspectives on management and administration. Chapter 13 consists of summary and conclusion. The book is supported with bibliography.

However, this book is not intended to be the last word. If the reader wishes to gain a further comprehensive knowledge and deep understanding of the subject matters, he or she is directed to consult scholastic work listed under bibliography and the author feels great pleasure in acknowledging his gratitude to all the authors and publishers of this scholastic work which some times consulted and quoted in the text of this book.

The author earnestly hopes that the matters raised in this book will help the general readers and academic students and scholars and other professional in understanding concepts and application of management, management principles and management process. Finally, the readers and the users of this book are cordially invited to point out errors/mistakes and forward their comments/suggestions, which may bring about improvement to the next edition of this publication.

Praised be to Allah, the Lord of the Worlds!

Dr Wazir Ali Khan
Senior Citizen of Pakistan and the United Kingdon
Advocate of Peace and Social Reforms Activist
Research Scientist, Author and Publisher
Uxbridge (85) UB7 8AB, London, United Kingdom
Email: drwakhan@aol.com
Published Books link:
http://www.amazon.co.uk/s/ref=nb_sb_noss?url=searc
h-alias%3Ddigital-text&field-keywords=Wazir+Khan

Chapter 1

INTRODCTION

For better or worse, our society is strongly influenced by managers and their organization where an organization is a group of two or more people working together in predetermined fashion to attain a set of goals. The goals may include successful completion of project, optimization of profit, the discovery of knowledge, national defence or co-ordination of various charities, etc. Since organizations play a significant role in people's lives, therefore, it is important to understand how organizations operate and how they are managed.

In the late 1800s , managerial function approach was the first systematic attempt to improve the leadership of organizations to systematise the process of getting things done by others. The earlier writers identifies the execution of six functions as the managerial roles, namely: (i) planning, (ii) organizing, (iii) staffing, (iv) motivating, (v) co-ordinating, and (vi) controlling. However, the Industrial revolution created large and complex organizations which in order to succeed demanded new direction of co-ordinating.

Managers, therefore believed that to achieve success they have to plan their action carefully, organize their available resources precisely, control behavior of their work-force closely, measure results accurately, and apply 'carrot and stick' approach i.e. rewards and punishment to motivate their employees. This functions approach dominated managerial practices throughout this century. However, the new competitive realities such as: globalisation, customer service, and work-force diversity, etc. require new response from managers/ leaders and new methods to guide their organizations.

Today centralised planning and controls are no longer adequate as planning needs to be flexible and dynamic and controlling needs to be decentralised down the organizational hierarchy as much as possible. Leading requires many diversified functions as effective results demand involving work-force in the work and providing employees with a say in what they do. Although the traditional carrot and stick approach in the form of pay and promotion continue to have influence, but nevertheless, this approach need to be supplemented by other incentives such as: participative management, management by objectives, etc thus giving the workers control over their work. Management is an activity concerned with guiding human and physical resources such that organizational goals can be achieved. In broad term, the nature of management can be considered in the following perspective: -

Management is Goal-Oriented: The success of any management activity is assessed by its achievement of the predetermined goals or objective. Management is a purposeful activity. It is a tool which helps use of human and physical resources to fulfill the pre-determined goals. For example, the goal of an enterprise is to maximise consumer satisfaction by producing quality goods and at reasonable prices. This can be achieved by employing efficient manpoer and making better use of scarce resources.

Management integrates Human, Physical and Financial Resources: In an organization, human beings work with non-human resources like machines. Materials, financial assets, buildings etc. Management integrates human efforts to those resources. It brings harmony among the human, physical and financial resources.

Management is Continuous: Management is an ongoing process. It involves continuous handling of problems and issues. It is concerned with identifying the problem and taking appropriate steps to solve it e.g. the target of a company is maximum production. For achieving this target various policies have to be framed but this is not the end as it requires marketing and advertising.

Management is all Pervasive: Management is required in all types of organizations whether it is political, social, cultural or business because it helps and directs various efforts towards a definite purpose. Thus hospitals, political parties, academic institutions, and business firms all require management. Whenever more than one person is engaged in working for a common goal, management becomes necessary. Whether it is a small business firm which may be engaged in trading or a large firm, management is required everywhere irrespective of size or type of activity.

Management is a Group Activity: Management is very much less concerned with individual's efforts. It is more concerned with groups. It involves the use of group effort to achieve predetermined goal of management of XYZ & Co. is good refers to a group of persons managing that enterprise.

Chapter 2

MANAGEMENT AND MANAGER DEFINED

2.1 WHAT IS MANAGEMENT?

2.1.1 General Defnition

Management is a universal phenomenon and is a very popular and widely used term. All organizations - business, political, cultural or social are involved in management because it is the management which helps and directs the various efforts towards a definite purpose. There are numerous definitions of management. Early writers on the subject defined management as 'knowing exactly what you want (people) to do, and then seeing that they do it in the best and cheapest way'. Jean-Jacques Servan-Schreiber describes management as 'Management is, all things, considered, the most creative of all arts. It is the art of arts, because it is the organizer of talent'.

According to Harold Koontz, "Management is an art of getting things done through and with the people in formally organized groups. It is an art of creating an environment in which people can perform and individuals can co-operate towards attainment of group goals". According to *F.W. Taylor*, "Management is an art of knowing what to do, when to do and see that it is done in the best and cheapest way". Management, in practice, is a very complex process and its definition needs to be developed, that better captures the true nature of that process.

Management is a purposive activity. It is something that directs group efforts towards the attainment of certain pre-determined goals. It is the process of working with and through others to effectively achieve the goals of the organization, by efficiently using limited resources in the changing world. Of course, these goals may vary from one enterprise to another, e.g. for one enterprise it may be launching of new products by conducting market surveys and for other it may be profit maximization by minimizing cost.

Management involves creating an internal environment, e.g. it is the management which puts into use the various factors of production. Therefore, it is the responsibility of management to create such conditions which are conducive to maximum efforts so that people are able to perform their task efficiently and effectively. It includes ensuring availability of raw materials, determination of wages and salaries, formulation of rules and regulations etc. Therefore, we can say that good management includes both being effective and efficient. Being effective means doing the appropriate task i.e, fitting the square pegs in square holes and round pegs in round holes and being efficient means doing the task correctly, at least possible cost with minimum wastage of resources.

2.1.2   Management as a Process

As a process, management refers to a series of inter-related functions. It is the process by which management creates, operates and directs purposive organization through systematic, coordinated and co-operated human efforts, according to George R. Terry, "Management is a distinct process consisting of planning, organizing, actuating and controlling, performed to determine and accomplish stated objective by the use of human beings and other resources". As a process, management consists of three aspects, namely: (i) Management is a social process - Since human factor is most important among the other factors, therefore management is concerned with developing relationship among people.

It is the duty of management to make interaction between people - productive and useful for obtaining organizational goals. (ii) Management is an integrating process - Management undertakes the job of bringing together human physical and financial resources so as to achieve organizational purpose. Therefore, is an important function to bring harmony between various factors. (iii) Management is a continuous (on-going) process - It is a never ending process. It is concerned with constantly identifying the problem and solving them by taking adequate steps. See Fig. 1.1.

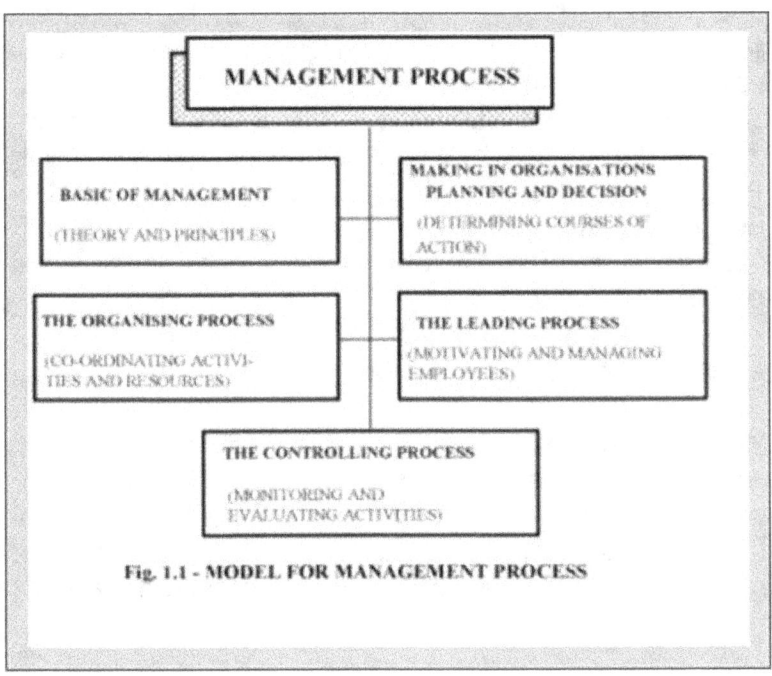

Fig. 1.1 - MODEL FOR MANAGEMENT PROCESS

2.1.3 Management as an Activity

Like various other activities performed by human beings such as writing, playing, eating, cooking etc, management is also an activity because a manager is one who accomplishes the objectives by directing the efforts of others. According to Koontz, "Management is what a manager does". Management as an activity includes: (i) Informational activities - In the functioning of business enterprise, the manager constantly has to receive and give information orally or in written. A communication link has to be maintained with subordinates as well as superiors for effective functioning of an enterprise. (ii) Decisional activities - Practically all types of managerial activities are based on one or the other types of decisions.

Therefore, managers are continuously involved in decisions of different kinds since the decision made by one manager becomes the basis of action to be taken by other managers. (iii) Inter-personal activities - Management involves achieving goals through people. Therefore, managers have to interact with super-ordinates as well as the sub-ordinates. They must maintain good relations with them. For example, the inter-personal activities with the sub-ordinates may include taking care of the problem - e.g. bonuses to be given to the sub-ordinates.

2.1.5   Management as a Discipline

Management as a discipline refers to that branch of knowledge which is connected to study of principles and practices of basic administration. It specifies certain code of conduct to be followed by the manager and also various methods for managing resources efficiently.

Management as a discipline indicates various methods of managing an enterprise.

Management is a course of study which is now formally being taught in the academic institutions, who after completing a prescribed course award degree or diploma in management, which helps a person to get employment as a manager. Any branch of knowledge that fulfils following two requirements is known as discipline: (a) there must be scholars and thinkers who communicate relevant knowledge through research and publications; and the knowledge should be formally imparted by education and training programmes. Accordingly, if management satisfies both these problems, it qualifies to be a discipline.

2.1.6   Management as a Group

Management as a group refers to all those persons who perform the task of managing an enterprise. For example, when we say that management of XYZ & Co. is good, we are referring to a group of people those who are managing that company. Thus as a group technically speaking, includes all managers from chief executive to the first-line managers (lower-level managers). But in common practice management includes only top management i.e. Chief Executive, Chairman, General Manager, Board of Directors etc. In other words, those who are concerned with making important decisions and enjoy the authorities to use resources to accomplish organizational objectives and also responsibility towards their efficient utilization.

Management as a group may be looked upon in two different ways, namely: (a) all managers taken together; and (b) only the top management. The interpretation depends upon the context in which these terms are used. Broadly speaking, there are three types of managers, namely: (i) Patrimonial/Family Manager -

those who have become managers by virtue of their being owners or relatives of the owners of company; (ii) Professional Managers - those who have been appointed on account of their specialized knowledge and degree quualification.; and (iii) Political Managers/Civil Servants: Those who manage public sector undertakings.

2.1.7 Management as both Science and Art

Management is both a science and an art. As we have earier discussed some points, which clearly reveal that management combines features of both science as well as art. It is considered as a science because it has an organized body of knowledge which contains certain universal truth. It is called an art because managing requires certain skills which are personal possessions of managers. Science provides the knowledge and art deals with the application of knowledge and skills.

A manager to be successful in his profession must acquire the knowledge of science and the art of applying it. Therefore management is a prudent blend of science as well as an art because it proves the principles and the way these principles are applied is a matter of art. Science teaches to 'know' and art teaches to 'do' e.g. a person cannot become a good project manager unless he has knowledge about various phases and scope of a project he also applies his personal skill in the art of managing all those phases suucessfully.

Same way it is not sufficient for manager to first know the principles but he must also apply them in solving various managerial problems that is why, science and art are not mutually exclusive but they are complementary to each other. The old saying that

"Manager are Born" has been rejected in favour of "Managers are Made". Therefore, it has been aptly remarked that management is the oldest of art and youngest of science.

MANAGEMENT AS A SCIENCE

As we are aware that science is a systematic body of knowledge pertaining to a specific field of study that contains general facts which explains a phenomenon, which establishes cause and effect relationship between two or more variables and underlines the principles governing their relationship. These principles are developed through scientific method of observation and verification through testing.

Science is characterized by main features, such as: (a) universally acceptance principles - scientific principles represents basic truth about a particular field of enquiry, which may be applied in all situations, at all time and at all places e.g. - law of gravitation which can be applied in all countries irrespective of the time; (b) management also contains some fundamental principles which can be applied universally like the Principle of Unity of Command i.e. one man, one boss. This principle is applicable to all type of organization - business or non business; and (c) experimentation and observation - scientific principles are derived through scientific investigation and researching i.e. they are based on logic e.g. the principle that earth goes round the sun has been scientifically proved.

Management principles are also based on scientific enquiry and observation and not only for example, on the opinion of Henry Fayol. They have been developed through experiments and practical experiences of large number of managers e.g. it is observed that fair remuneration to personal helps in creating a satisfied work force. Principles of science lay down cause and effect relationship between various variables. e.g. when metals are heated, they are expanded.

The cause is heating and effect (result) is expansion. The same is true for management, therefore it also establishes cause and effect relationship, e.g. lack of parity (balance) between authority and responsibility will lead to ineffectiveness. If you know the cause i.e. lack of balance, the effect can be ascertained easily i.e. in effectiveness. Similarly if workers are given bonuses, fair wages they will work hard but when not treated in fair and just manner, reduces productivity of organization.

Validity of scientific principles can be tested at any time or any number of times i.e. they stand the test of time. Each time these tests will give similar result. Also, future events can be predicted with reasonable accuracy by using scientific principles, e.g. H_2 and O_2 will always give H_2O. Likewise, Principles of management can be tested for validity, e.g. principle of unity of command can be tested by comparing two persons - one having single boss and one having 2 bosses. The performance of 1st person will be better than 2nd.

Although, management has a systematic body of knowledge but nevertheless it is not as exact as that of other physical sciences like mathematics, biology, physics, and chemistry etc. The main reason for the inexactness of science of management is that it deals with human beings and it is very difficult to predict their behaviour accurately. Since it is a social process, therefore it falls in the area of social sciences. It is a flexible science and that is why its theories and principles may produce different results at different times and therefore it is a behaviour science.

MANAGEMENT AS AN ART

Management as an art implies application of knowledge and skill to trying for desired results. An art may be defined as personalized application of general theoretical principles for achieving best possible results. Art's characters include but not limited to:

Creativity: Every artist has an element of creativity in line. That is why he aims at producing something that has never existed before which requires combination of intelligence & imagination. Management is also creative in nature like any other art. It combines human and non-human resources in useful way so as to achieve desired results. It tries to produce sweet music by combining chords in an efficient manner.

Practical Knowledge: Every art requires practical knowledge therefore learning of theory is not sufficient. It is very important to know practical application of theoretical principles. E.g. to become a good painter, the person may not only be knowing different colour and brushes but different designs, dimensions, situations etc to use them appropriately. A manager can never be successful just by obtaining degree or diploma in management; he must have also know how to apply various principles in real situations by functioning in capacity of manager.

Personal Skill: Although theoretical base may be same for every artist, but each one has his own style and approach towards his job. That is why the level of success and quality of performance differs from one person to another. E.g. there are several qualified painters but M.F. Hussain is recognized for his style. Similarly management as an art is also personalized.

Every manager has his own way of managing things based on his knowledge, experience and personality, that is why some managers are known as good managers (like Aditya Birla, Rahul Bajaj) whereas others as bad.

Perfection through practice: Practice makes a man perfect. Every artist becomes more and more proficient through constant practice. Similarly managers learn through an art of trial and error initially but application of management principles over the years makes them perfect in the job of managing.

Goal-Oriented: Every art is result oriented as it seeks to achieve concrete results. In the same manner, management is also directed towards accomplishment of pre-determined goals. Managers use various resources like men, money, material, machinery & methods to promote growth of an organization.

Therefore, we can deduce that management is an art as not only it requires application of certain principles but also it is an art of highest order because it deals with moulding the behaviour and attitude of people at work towards desired goals.

2.1.8 Management as a Profession

Factors such as growing size of business unit, separation of ownership from management, growing competition etc, over a few decades, have led to an increased demand for professionally qualified managers as the task of manager has been quite specialized in nature. As a result of these developments the management has reached a stage where everything is to be managed professionally. In this context, a profession may be defined as an occupation that requires specialized knowledge and intensive academic preparations to which entry is regulated by a representative body. The essentials of a profession includes bt not limited to the following:

Specialized Knowledge - A profession must have a systematic body of knowledge that can be used for development of professionals. Every professional must make deliberate efforts to acquire expertise in the principles and techniques. Similarly a manager must have devotion and involvement to acquire expertise in the science of management.

Formal Education & Training - There are no. of institutes and universities to impart education & training for a profession. No one can practice a profession without going through a prescribed course. Many institutes of management have been set up for imparting education and training. For example, a CA cannot audit the A/C's unless he has acquired a degree or diploma for the same but no minimum qualifications and a course of study has been prescribed for managers by law. For example, MBA may be preferred but not necessary.

Representative Association - For the regulation of profession, existance of a representative body is a must. For example, an institute of management (previously known as British Institute of Management) establishes and administers standards of competence and regulate the activities of managers.

Social Obligations - Profession is a source of livelihood but professionals are primarily motivated by the desire to serve the society. Their actions are influenced by social norms and values. Similarly a manager is responsible not only to its owners but also to the society and therefore he is expected to provide quality goods at reasonable prices to the society.

Code of Conduct - Members of a profession have to abide by a code of conduct which contains certain rules and regulations, norms of honesty, integrity and special ethics. A code of conduct is enforced by a representative association to ensure self discipline among its members. Any member violating the code of conduct can be punished and his membership can be withdrawn.

From above discussion, it is evident that management fulfills several essentials of a profession, but it is not a full fledged profession because: (a) it does not restrict the entry in managerial jobs for account of one standard or other; (b) no minimum qualifications have been prescribed for managers; (c) no management association has the authority to grant a certificate of practice to various managers. (d) all managers are supposed to abide by the code formulated by the professional body; (e) competent education and training facilities do not exist; (f) managers are responsible to many groups such as shareholders, employees and society. A regulatory code may curtail their freedom; (g) managers are known by their performance and not mere degrees; (h) the ultimate goal of business is to maximize profit and not social welfare. That is why Haymes has rightly remarked, "The slogan for management is becoming - 'He who serves best, also profits most'."

2.2   MANAGER DEFINED

Systems Theory suggests that organization utilise four basic kinds of resources (inputs) i.e., Human,

Monetary, Physical and Information. The Manager's task involves combining and co-ordinating these resources to achieve the organization's goals, by carrying out four basic managerial functions, namely: Planning and Decision Making, Organizing, Leading, and Controlling. Therefore, in the light of System Theory the management can be defined as follows: *'Management is the process of planning and decision making, organizing, leading, and controlling an organization's human, financial, physical and information resources to achieve organizational goals in an efficient and effective manner'.* Under this concept, manager can be defined in the following words: 'A manager is someone who plans and makes decisions, organizes, leads and controls human, financial, physical, and information resources of his respective organization'.

Chapter 3

PRINCIPLES OF MANAGEMENT

3.1 INTRODUCTION

A principle refers to a fundamental truth. It establishes cause and effect relationship between two or more variables under given situation. They serve as a guide to thought & actions. Therefore, management principles are the statements of fundamental truth based on logic which provides guidelines for managerial decision making and actions. These principles are derived: (a) On the basis of observation and analysis i.e. practical experience of managers; (b by conducting experimental studies.

3.2 HANRI FAYOL'S PRINCIPLES OF MANAGEMENT

There are 14 Principles of Management described by Henri Fayol. See Fig. 1.2.

1. Division of Labor

Henry Fayol has stressed on the specialization of jobs and recommended that work of all kinds must be divided and subdivided and allotted to various persons according to their expertise in a particular area, where specialization leads to efficiency and economy in spheres of business, whilst subdivision of work makes it simpler and results in efficiency and also helps the individual in acquiring speed, accuracy in his performance.

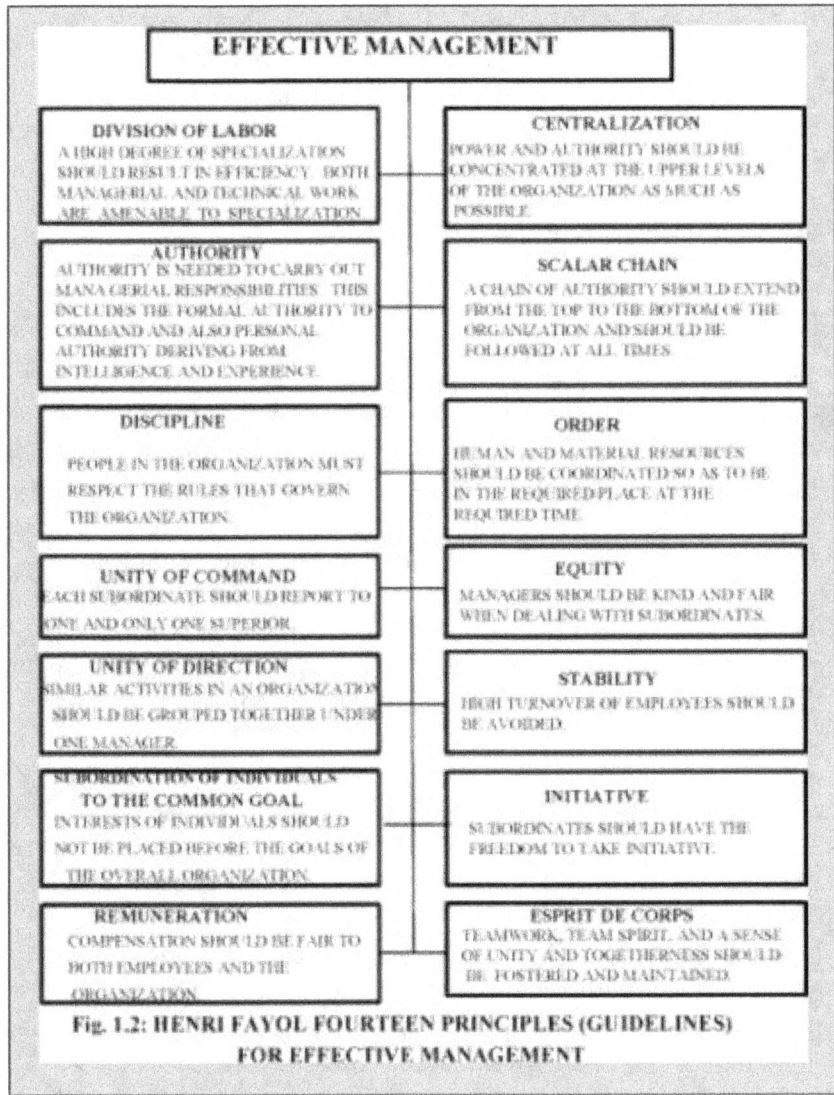

Fig. 1.2: HENRI FAYOL FOURTEEN PRINCIPLES (GUIDELINES) FOR EFFECTIVE MANAGEMENT

2. Authority And Responsibility

Authority and responsibility are co-existing entities and there should be a balance between the two i.e. they must go hand in hand. If authority is given to a person, he should also be made responsible. In a same way, if anyone is made responsible for any job, he should also have concerned authority. Here authority refers to the right of superiors to get exactness from their sub-ordinates whereas responsibility means obligation for the performance of the job assigned. Responsibility without authority makes the person ineffective, wheras authority without responsibility leads to irresponsible behavior.

3. Discipline

According to Fayol, "Discipline means sincerity, obedience, respect of authority & observance of rules and regulations of the enterprise". This principle applies that subordinates should respect their superiors and obey their order, believing that it is an important requisite for smooth running of the enterprise. Discipline is not only required on part of subordinates but also on the part of management. Discipline can be enforced if, (a)there are good superiors at all levels; there are clear and fair agreements with workers; and sanctions (punishments) are applied judiciously.

4. Unity of Command: Principle of One Boss

Unity of command provides the enterprise a disciplined, stable and orderly existence and it creates harmonious relationship between superiors and sub-ordinates. A sub-ordinate should receive orders and be accountable to one and only one boss at a time. In other words, a sub-ordinate should not receive instructions from more than one person because: it undermines authority; weakens discipline; divides loyalty; creates confusion; results in delays and chaos; result in escaping responsibilities; it results in duplication of work; it results in overlapping of efforts. Therefore, dual sub-ordination should be avoided unless and until it is absolutely essential.

5. Unity of Direction

Fayol advocates one head one plan which means that there should be one plan for a group of activities having similar objectives and related activities should be grouped together. There should be one plan of action for them and they should be under the charge of a particular manager. According to this principle, efforts of all the members of the organization should be directed towards the common goal. Unity of command is not possible without unity of direction and without unity of direction, unity of action cannot be achieved. The unity of direction and the unity of command fifer in meaning, natre, necessity, advantage and result. See Fig. 1.2a.

BASIS	UNITY OD DIRECTION	UNITY OF COMMAND
Meaning	It means one head, one plan for a group of activities having similar objectives.	It implies that a sub-ordinate should receive orders & instructions from only one boss.
Nature	It is related to the functioning of departments, or organization as a whole.	It is related to the functioning of personnel.
Necessity	It is necessary for sound organization.	It is necessary for fixing responsibility of each of the sub-ordinates.
Advantage	It avoids duplication of efforts and wastage of resources.	It avoids conflicts, confusion and chaos.
Result	It leads to smooth running of the enterprise.	It leads to better superior sub-ordinate relationship.

Fig. 1.2a

It is obvious that unity of direction and unity of command are different from each other but they are dependent on each other i.e. unity of direction is a pre-requisite for unity of command. Unity of direction, however, does not automatically comes from the unity of direction.

6. Common Goal

Interet of the individuals (management or workers) should be place before the I goal of the overall operations.

7. Fair Remuneration

The quantum and method of remuneration to be paid to the workers should be fair, reasonable, satisfactory and rewarding of the efforts. As far as possible it should accord satisfaction to both employer and the employees. Wages should be determined on the basis of wage rate prevailing, cost of living, work assigned, financial position of the business, etc. Logical and appropriate wage rates and methods of their payment reduce tension and differences between workers and management creates harmonious relationship and pleasing atmosphere of work. In this context, Fayol recommended provision of other benefits such as free education, medical, housing or housing allowance to workers.

8. Centralization And De-Centralization

Centralization means concentration of authority at the top level. In other words, centralization is a situation in which top management retains most of the decision making authority. Decentralization means disposal of decision making authority to all the levels of the organization. In other words, sharing authority downwards is decentralization. According to Fayol, "Degree of centralization or decentralization depends on number of factors like: size of business; experience of superiors; dependability and ability of subordinates etc. Anything which increases the role of subordinate is decentralization and anything which decreases it is centralization. Fayol suggested that absolute centralization or decentralization is not feasible. An organization should strike to achieve a lot between the two.

9. Scalar Chain

Fayol defines scalar chain as 'The chain of superiors ranging from the ultimate authority to the lowest". Every orders, instructions, messages, requests, explanation etc. has to pass through Scalar chain. But, for the sake of convenience and urgency, this path can be cut shirt and this short cut is known as Gang Plank. A Gang Plank is a temporary arrangement between two different points to facilitate quick and easy communication as explained in Fig. 1.2b.

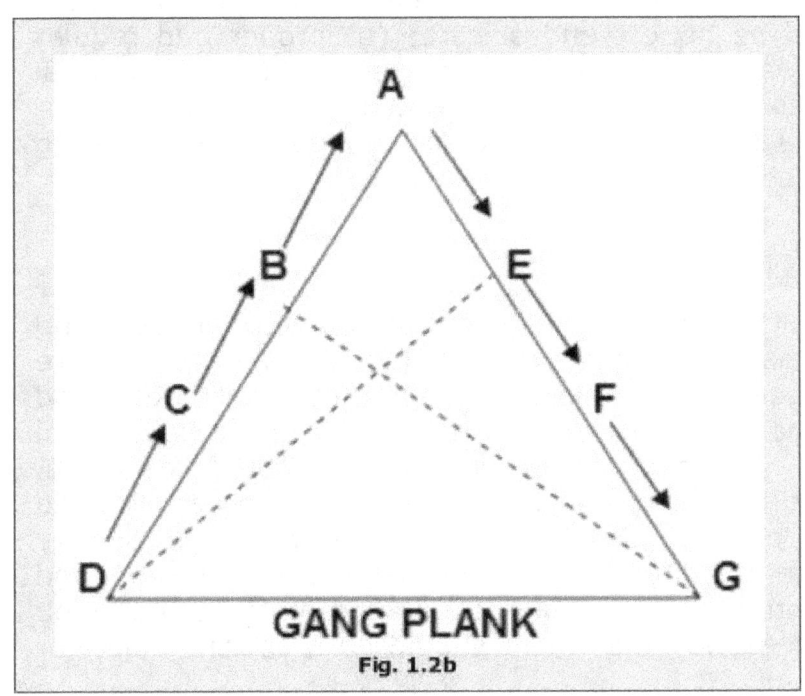

GANG PLANK

Fig. 1.2b

In the figure given, if D has to communicate with G he will first send the communication upwards with the help of C, B to A and then downwards with the help of E and F to G which will take quite some time and by that time, it may not be worth therefore a gang plank has been developed between the two. Gang Plank clarifies that management principles are not rigid rather they are very flexible. They can be moulded and modified as per the requirements of situations.

Sub-Ordination of Individual Interest to General Interest. An organization is much bigger than the individual it constitutes therefore interest of the undertaking should prevail in all circumstances. As far as possible, reconciliation should be achieved between individual and group interests, but in case of conflict, individual must sacrifice for bigger interests. In order to achieve this attitude, it is essential that: (a) employees should be honest and sincere; (b) proper and regular supervision of work; and (c) reconciliation of mutual differences and clashes by mutual agreement, e.g. for change of location of plant, for change of profit sharing ratio, etc.

10. Order

This principle is concerned with proper and systematic arrangement of things and people, where arrangement of things is called material order and arrangement (placement) of people is called social order. In aaterial order, there should be safe, appropriate and specific place for every article and every place to be effectively used for specific activity and commodity; whilst in social order, selection and appointment of most suitable person on the suitable job in suchas way that there should be a specific place for every one and everyone should have a specific place so that they can easily be contacted whenever need arises.

11. Equity

Equity means combination of fairness, kindness & justice, therefore, the employees should be treated with kindness and equity if devotion is expected of them. It implies that managers should be fair and impartial while dealing with the subordinates and should extend similar treatment to people of similar position. They should not discriminate with respect to age, caste, sex, religion, relation etc.

Equity is essential to create and maintain cordial relations between the managers and sub-ordinate, but equity does not mean total absence of harshness. Fayol was of opinion that, "at times force and harshness might become necessary for the sake of equity".

12. Stability od Tenure

Fayol emphasized that employees should not be moved frequently from one job position to another i.e. the period of service in a job should be fixed. Therefore employees should be appointed after keeping in view principles of recruitment and selection but once they are appointed their services should be served.

According to Fayol. "Time is required for an employee to get used to a new work & succeed to doing it well but if he is removed before that he will not be able to render worthwhile services", resulting in the time, effort and money spent on training the worker will go waste. Stability of job creates team spirit and a sense of belongingness among workers which in turn ultimately increase the quantity as well as quality of work.

13. Initiative

Workers should be encouraged to take initiative in the work assigned to them. It means eagerness to initiate actions without being asked to do so. Fayol advised that management should provide opportunity to its employees to suggest ideas, experiences and new method of work as it would help in developing an atmosphere of trust and understanding and at the same time People would enjoy working in the organization because it adds to their zeal and energy. The people should be motivated and encourages by providing monetary and non-monetary incentives.

14. Espirit De' Corps

Thia can be achieved through unity of command.It refers to team spirit i.e. harmony in the work groups and mutual understanding among the members. Spirit De' Corps inspires workers to work harder. Fayol cautioned the managers against dividing the employees into competing groups because it might damage the moral of the workers and interest of the undertaking in the long run. To inculcate Espirit De' Corps following steps should be undertaken: (i)There should be proper co-ordination of work at all levels. (ii) Subordinates should be encouraged to develop informal relations among themselves. (iii) Efforts should be made to create enthusiasm and keenness among subordinates so that they can work to the maximum ability. (iv) Efficient employees should be rewarded and those who are not up to the mark should be given a chance to improve their performance. (v) Subordinates should be made conscious of that whatever they are doing is of great importance to the business & society.

Fayol also cautioned against the more use of Britain communication to the subordinates i.e. face to face communication should be developed. The managers should infuse team spirit and belongingness. There should be no place for misunderstanding. People then enjoy working in the organization and offer their best towards the organization.

3.5   FEATURES OF PRINCIPLES OF MANAGEMENT

Principles of Management are Universal as these are applicable to all kinds of organizations (business and non business) and to all levels of management. Every organization must make best possible use by the use of management principles. Therefore, they are universal or all pervasive.

Principles of Management are Flexible as these are dynamic guidelines and not static rules, therefore, here is sufficient room for managerial discretion i.e. they can be modified as per the requirements of the situation, whist modification and improvement is a continuous phenomenon.

Principles of Management have a Cause and Effect Relationship as hese indicate cause and effect relationship between related variables. They indicate what will be the consequence or result of certain actions, therefore, if one is known, the other can be traced.

Principles of Management aims at Influencing Human Behavior as human behavior is complex and unpredictable. Management principles are directed towards regulating human behavior so that people can give their best to the organization. Management is concerned with integrating efforts and harmonizing them towards a goal, but in certain situations even these principles fail to understand human behavior.

Principles of Management are of Equal Importance as no particular principle has greater importance than the other. They are all required together for the achievement of organizational goals.

3.6 IMPORTANCE OF THE PRINCIPLES OF MANAGEMENT

The principal important domains of the Principles of Management includes but not limited to: Role of Management; Direction for Training of Managers; Improves Understanding; and Guide to Research in Management.

Role of Management - Management principles makes the role of manager concrete. Therefore these principles act as ready reference to the managers to check whether their decisions are appropriate. Besides these principles, managerial activities in practical terms tell what a manager is expected to do in specific situation.

Direction for Training of Managers - Principles of management provide understanding of management process what managers would do to accomplish what. Thus, these are helpful in identifying the areas of management in which existing and future managers should be trained and developed.

Improves Understanding - From the knowledge of principles managers get indication on how to manage an organization. The principles enable managers to decide what should be done to accomplish given tasks and to handle situations which may arise in management. These principles make managers more efficient in their role.

Guide to Research in Management - The body of management principles indicate lines along which research should be undertaken to make management practical and more effective. For example, the principles of management guide managers in decision making and action and enabe them to examine whether the guidelines are useful or not. Anything which makes management research more exact,pointed and targeted which in turm will help improve management practice.

Chapter 4

LEVELS AND AREAS OF MANAGEMENT

4.1 INTRODUCTION

There are various levels of management as well as areas of management depending upon the nature and size of the enterprise. The common view on the level of management is that there are three basic levels, i.e., top management, middle management and first-line management. The top management consists of top executives who control the organization, e.g. President, Vice President, Managing Director, Chief Executive, etc. Top management establishes the organizational goals, overall strategy and operational policies of the enterprise. Middle managers are often innovators. The middle management consists of Executive Managers, who implement the policies and plans developed by the top management, e.g., Operations Manager, Engineering Managers, Plant Manager or other Department Heads, etc.

Major responsibility of Middle Managers is to supervise and control the activities of the first-line managers. The first-line managers supervise and co-ordinate the activities of operating supervisors and employees, e.g., foremen, section supervisors, office managers, etc. Depending upon the nature of the enterprise, areas of management may differ e.g., marketing, financial, personnel, administrative, operations, etc. Managers at different levels may function in various areas within the same organization.

4.2   PRINCIPAL OBJECTIVES OF MANAGEMENT

The principal objectives of management include but not limited to the following:

To act as Ambassadors of Goodwill for the Enterprise: Websters Online Dictionary presents a specialty definition for a goodwill ambassador as one that promotes goodwill and solicits trade for local business firms who are members of parent organization: Develops list of prospective clients from such sources as newspaper items, utility companies' records, and local merchants. Goodwill ambassadors generally deliver goodwill or promote ideals from one entity or enterprize to another, or to shareholdera as for that matter to the general population.

Getting Maximum Results with Minimum Efforts: The main objective of management is to secure optimm outputs with minimum efforts and resources. Management is basically concerned with thinking and utilizing human, material and financial resources in such a manner that would result in best combination in maximizing the profitability of the enterprise and in reducinf various costs.

Human betterment and Social Justice: Management serves as a tool for the upliftment as well as betterment of the society. Through increased productivity and employment as management ensures better standards of living for the society and It provides justice through its uniform policies.

Increasing the Efficiency of factors of Production: Through proper utilization of various factors of production the efficiency can be increased to a great extent which can be obtained by reducing spoilage, wastages and breakage of all kinds, this in turn leads to saving of time, effort and money which is essential for the growth and prosperity of the enterprise.

Maximum Prosperity for Employer and Employees: Management ensures smooth and coordinated functioning of the enterprise. This in turn helps in providing maximum benefits in kind to the employee, such as: good working condition; suitable wage system; and incentive plans on the one hand and higher profits to the employer on the other hand.

4.3   LEVELS OF MANAGEMENT

The term "Levels of Management' refers to a line of demarcation between various managerial positions in an organization. The number of levels in management increases when the size of the business and work force increases and decreases when size and workforce decreases. The level of management determines a chain of command, the amount of authority, and status enjoyed by any managerial position. The levels of management can be classified in three broad categories, namely: (a) top level management; (b) middle level management; and low level management. Managers at all these levels perform different functions. See Fig 1.2c. The role of the manager in these levels of management are discussed herein below:

4.3.1 Top Level of Management

It consists of: board of directors; chief executive or managing director. The top management manages goals and policies for an enterprise and is the ultimate source of authority. It devotes more time on proactive planning and coordinating functions.

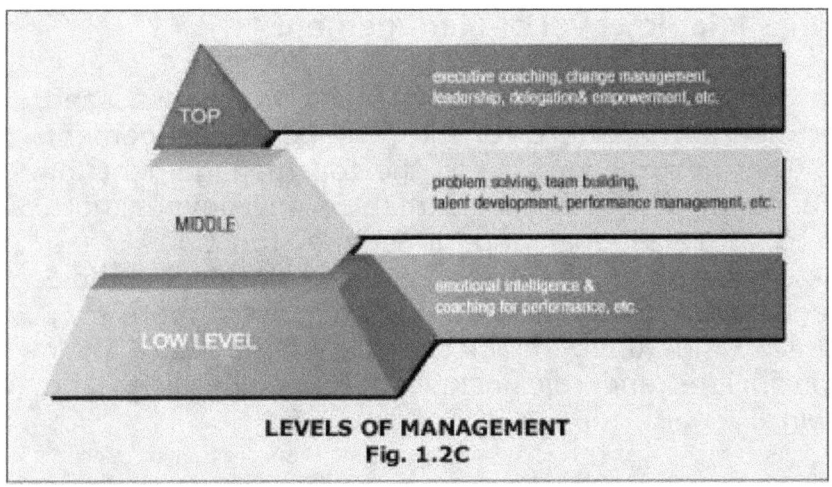

executive coaching, change management, leadership, delegation & empowerment, etc.

TOP

problem solving, team building, talent development, performance management, etc.

MIDDLE

emotional intelligence & coaching for performance, etc.

LOW LEVEL

LEVELS OF MANAGEMENT
Fig. 1.2C

The responsibilities and role of the top management include but not limited to the following:

i.   The top management is responsible towards the shareholders for the performance of the enterprise.

ii.   The top management is also responsible for maintaining a contact with the outside world.

iii.   The top management lays down the objectives and broad policies of the enterprise.

iv.   The top management issues necessary instructions for preparation of department budgets, procedures, schedules etc.

v.   The top management prepares strategic policies and plans for the enterprise.

vi.   Top management appoints the executive for middle level i.e. departmental managers.

vii.   The top management controls and coordinates the activities of all the departments.

viii. The top management provides guidance and direction and issue directives from time to time.

ix.   The top management carries out other function as deemed necessary as approved by the Board.

4.3.4   Middle Level of Management

By and large, the branch managers and departmental managers constitute middle management level. They are responsible to the top management for the functioning of their department. They devote more time to organizational and directional functions. In a small organization there is only one layer of middle management level wheras in big enterprises, there may be senior and junior middle level management. Their responsibilities and role include but not limited to the following:

i.   By and large middle management is responsible for profit and loss in their area of operation'
ii.   The middle management is also responsible for inspiring lower level managers towards better performance.
iii. The middle management executes the plans of the organization in accordance with the policies and directives of the top management.
iv.   The middle management makes plans for the sub-units of the organization.
v.   The middle management participates in employment and training of lower level management.
vi.   The middle management interprets and explains policies from top level management to lower level.
vii. The middle management is responsible for coordinating the activities within the division or department.
viii. The middle management evaluates performance of junior managers.
ix.   The middle management sends important reports and other important data to top level management.

x.   The middle management carries out other special tasks as deemed necessary by the top management.

4.3.5   Lower Level of Management

Lower level (also known as supervisory or operative level of management) consists of supervisors, foreman, section officers, superintendent, graduate trainees, etc. The low level management isconcerned with directional and controlling function of management. According to *R.C. Davis*: "supervisory management refers to those executives whose work has to be largely with personal oversight and direction of operative employees". The responsibilities, role and activities of low level management include but noe limited to the following:

i.   The lower level management is entrusted with the responsibility of maintaining good relation within the organization.
ii.   The lower level management is responsible for the quality as well as quantity of production.
iii. The lower level management is responsible for providing training to the workers.
iv.   The lower level management is the image builders of the enterprise because it is in direct contact with the workers.
v.   The lower level management assigns jobs and tasks to various workers.
vi.   The lower level management guides and instructs workers for day to day activities.
vii. The lower level management communicates workers problems, suggestions, and recommendatory appeals etc. to the higher level management.
viii. The lower level management also communicates higher level goals and objectives to the workers under its control.

ix.   The lower level management helps to solve the grievances of the workers.

x.   The lower level management supervises and guides the sub-ordinates.

xi.   The lower level management ensures discipline in the enterprise.

xii.   The lower level management arranges necessary labor, materials, machines, tools etc. for getting the things done.

xiii.   The lower level management motivates workers.

xiv.   The lower level management prepares periodical reports about the performance of the workers and submit to higher management.

4. 4   AREAS OF MANAGEMENT

The major areas of management include bt not limited to the following:

➢ Supply Chain Management
➢ Creative Production
➢ Purchasing
➢ Distibution
➢ Retailing
➢ Construction
➢ Media Management
➢ Customer Relationship Management
➢ Industrial Marketing
➢ Sales Marketing
➢ Advertising Research
➢ Advertising
➢ Export Marketing
➢ Brand Marketing
➢ Consumer Behavior
➢ Services Marketing
➢ Hman Resources Marketing

- ➢ International Marketing Communication
- ➢ Marketing Information System
- ➢ Seminar in Marketing

Chapter 5

IMPORTANCE AND SIGNIFICANCE OF MANAGEMENT

According to **Peter Drucker**: "Management is what the modern world is all about." This statement implies that all the development that has taken place in the world is due to efficient management. The salient points that bring out the **significance** or importance of management are shown in Fig. 1.2d and discussed herein below.

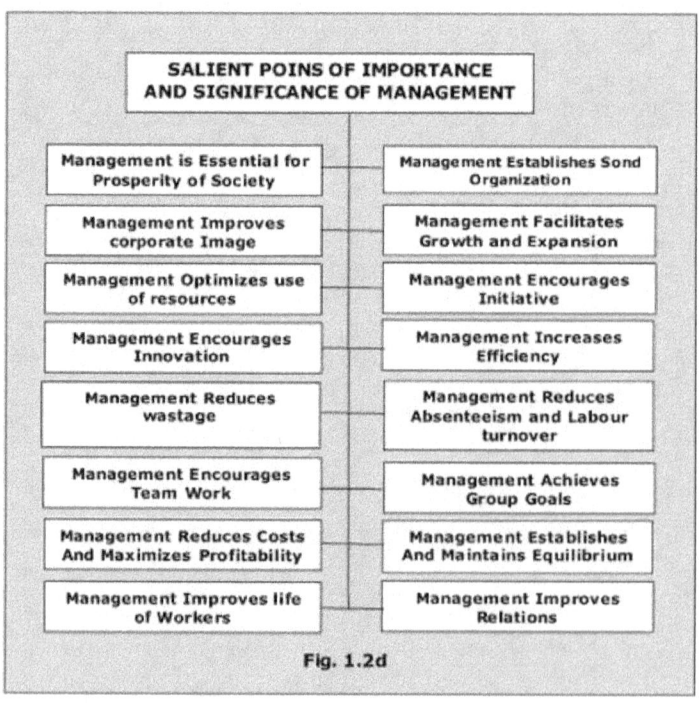

Fig. 1.2d

Management is Essential for Prosperity of Society: Efficient management leads to better economical production which helps in turn to increase the welfare of people. Good management makes a difficult task easier by avoiding wastage of scarce resource. It improves standard of living. It increases the profit which is beneficial to business and society will get maximum output at minimum cost by creating employment opportunities which generate income in hands. Organization comes with new products and researches beneficial for society.

Management Establishes Sond Organization: No overlapping of efforts (smooth and coordinated functions). To establish sound organizational structure is one of the objective of management which is in tune with objective of organization and for fulfillment of this, it establishes effective authority & responsibility relationship i.e. who is accountable to whom, who can give instructions to whom, who are superiors & who are subordinates. Management fills up various positions with right persons, having right skills, training and qualification. All jobs should be cleared to everyone.

Management Improves corporate Image: If the management is good, then the organisation will produce good quality goods and services. This will improve the goodwill and corporate image of the organisation. A good corporate image brings many added benefits to the organisation.

Management Facilitates Growth and Expansion: Management makes optimum utilisation of available resources. It reduces wastage and increase efficiency. It encourages team work and motivates employees. It also reduces absenteeism and labour turnover. All this results in growth, expansion and diversification of the organisation.

Management Optimizes use of resources: Management brings together the available resources. It makes optimum (best) use of these resources. This brings best results to the organisation. Management utilizes all the physical and human resources productively. This leads to efficacy in management. Management provides maximum utilization of scarce resources by selecting its best possible alternate use in industry from out of various uses. It makes use of experts, professional and these services leads to use of their skills, knowledge, and proper utilization and avoids wastage. If employees and machines are producing its maximum there is no under employment of any resources.

Management Encourages Initiative: Management encourages initiative. Initiative means to do the right thing at the right time without being told or influenced by the superior. The employees should be encouraged to make their own plans and also to implement these plans. Initiative gives satisfaction to employees and success to organisation.

Management Encourages Innovation: Management encourages innovation in the organisation. **Innovation** brings new ideas, new technology, new methods, new products, new services, etc. This makes the organisation more competitive and efficient.

Management Motivates Employees: Management motivates employees by providing financial and non-financial incentives. These incentives increase the willingness and efficiency of the employees. This results in boosting productivity and profitability of the organisation.

48

Management Increases Efficiency: Efficiency is the relationship between returns and cost. Management uses many techniques to increase returns and to reduce costs. Higher efficiency brings many benefits to the organisation.

Management Reduces wastage: Management reduces the wastage of human, material and financial resources. Wastage is reduced by proper production planning and control. If wastage is reduced then productivity will increase.

Management Reduces Absenteeism and Labour turnover: Absenteeism means the employee is absent without permission, whilst Labour Turnover means the employee leaves the organization. Labour absenteeism and turnover increases the cost and causes many problems in the smooth functioning of the organisation. Management uses different techniques to reduce absenteeism and labour turnover in the organisation.

Management Encourages Team Work: Management encourages employees to work as a team. It develops a team spirit in the organisation. This unity bring success to the organization.

Management Achieves Group Goals: It arranges the factors of production, assembles and organizes the resources, integrates the resources in effective manner to achieve goals. It directs group efforts towards achievement of pre-determined goals. By defining objective of organization clearly there would be no wastage of time, money and effort. Management converts disorganized resources of men, machines, money etc. into useful enterprise. These resources are coordinated, directed and controlled in such a manner that enterprise work towards attainment of goals.

Management Reduces Costs And Maximizes Profitability: It gets maximum results through minimum input by proper planning and by using minimum input & getting maximum output. Management uses physical, human and financial resources in such a manner which results in best combination. This helps in cost reduction.

Management Establishes and Maintains Equilibrium: It enables the organization to survive in changing environment. It keeps in touch with the changing environment. With the change is external environment, the initial co-ordination of organization must be changed. So it adapts organization to changing demand of market / changing needs of societies. It is responsible for growth and survival of organization.

Management Improves life of Workers: Management shares some of its profits with the workers. It provides the workers with good working environment and conditions. It also gives the workers many financial and non-financial incentives. All this improves the quality of life of the workers.

Management Improves Relations: Management improves relations between individuals, groups, departments and between levels of management. Better relations lead to better team work. Better team work brings success to the organisation.

Chapter 6

ASMINISTRATION VS MANAGEMENTS

Administration primarily means overall determination of policies. It refers to the activities of higher level. It lays down basic principles of the enterprise. According to Theo Haimann: "Administration means overall determination of policies, setting of major objectives, the identification of general purposes and laying down of broad programmes and projects", whilst according to Newman: "Administration means guidance, leadership and control of the efforts of the groups towards some common goals".

On the other hand, management is an art of getting things done through and with the people in formally organized groups. It involves conceiving, initiating and bringing together the various elements, such as: actuating; coordinating; and integrating the diverse organizational components while sustaining the viability of the organization towards some pre-determined goals.

The difference between Management and Administration can be summarized under 2 categories, namely: (a) Functions; and (b) Applicability/Usage. On the Basis of Functions is shown in Fig. 1.2e and On the Basis of Usage is shown in Fig. 1.2f.

BASES	ADMINISTRATION	MANAGEMENT
LEVEL	Top level function	Middle and lower level function
MEANING	It is concerned with formulation of policies, broad objectives, and plans.	Management is an art of getting things done through others by directing their efforts towards achievement of pre-determined goals.
SKILL	Conceptual and Human skills	Technical and Human skills
PROCES	Administration decides what is to be done and when it is to be done.	Management decides who should as it and how should he dot it.
FUNCTION	Administration is a thinking function because policies and plans are formulated and maintained under it.	Management is a doing function because managers get work done under their supervision.
NATURE	Administration is a decision-making functional nature.	Management is an executing function.

Fig. 1.2e

BASES	ADMINISTRATION	MANAGEMENT
APPLIABILITY	It is applicable to non-business concerns, i.e. hospitals, clubs, academic institutions etc.	It is applicable to business concerns i.e. profit-making organization.
INFLUENCE	The administration is influenced by public opinion, governmental policies, religious organizations, customs etc.	The management decisions are influenced by the values, opinions, beliefs and decisions of the managers.
STATUS	Administration represents owners of the enterprise who earn return on their capital invested & profits in the form of dividend.	Management is an executing function. Management constitutes the employees of the organization who are paid remuneration (in the form of salaries and wages).

Fig. 1.2f

In practice there is no difference between administration and management since every manager is concerned with both (i.e. administrative management function and operative management function) as shown in the Fig. 1.2g, which clearly shows degree of administration and management performed by the different levels of management. However, the managers who are higher up in the management hierarchy denote more time on administrative function and the lower level denote more time on directing and controlling worker's performance i.e. management.

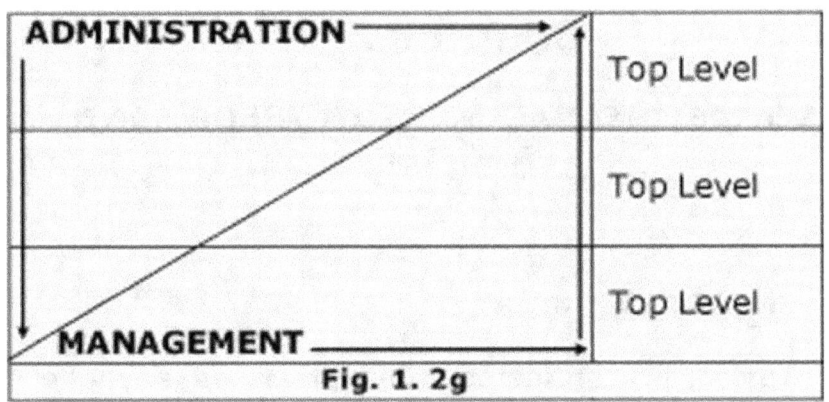

Fig. 1. 2g

Chapter 7

SCIENTIFIC MANAGEMENT IN THEORY AND PRACTICE

7.1   INTODUCTION

Taylor is considered the father of scientific management.[1] Taylorism's alternative view, however, considers, as the first form of scientific management, which was followed by new iterations. Therefore, in today's management theory, Taylorism is sometimes called (or considered a subset of) the classical perspective[2] of scientific management. Taylor's own early names for his approach included "shop management" and "process management". When Louis Brandeis popularized the term "scientific management" in 1910,[3]

Taylor recognized it as another good name for the concept, and he used it himself in his 1911 monograph. The fied of scientific management com comprised the

---

[1] Rosen, Ellen (1993), Improving Public Sector Productivity: Concepts and Practice, Thousand Oaks, CA, USA: Sage Publications, ISBN 978-0-8039-4573-9. This book on page 139quote: The worker was taken for granted as a cog in the machinery. The pioneers in diagnosing and prescribing for modern work organizations early in this century began with that very viewpoint. Frederick Taylor, father of scientific management, was an engineer; so was Henri Fayol, the early proponent of general principles of management.

[2] This means a perspective that's still respected for its seminal influence although it is no longer state-of-the-art.

[3] Drury, Horace Bookwalter (1915), 'Scientific management :a history and criticism', New York, NY, USA: Columbia University,pp. 15-21.

work of Taylor and his disciples, such as: Henry Gantt; Benjamin S. Graham; and Max Weber. It is compared and contrasted with other efforts, including those of Henri Fayol, Frank Gilbreth, Sr. and Lillian Moller Gilbreth. The proper Taylorism, in its strict sense, became obsolete by the 1930s, and by the 1960s the term "scientific management" had fallen out of favour for describing current management theories.

However, many *aspects* of scientific management have never stopped being part of later management efforts called by other names. There is no simple dividing line demarcating the time when management as a modern profession (blending art, academic science, and applied science) diverged from proper Taylorism. It was a gradual process that began as soon as Taylor published (as evidenced by e.g., Hartness's motivation to publish his *Human Factor*, or the Gilbreths' work). Each subsequent decade brought further evolution.

7.1   INTODUCTION

7.2   WHAT IS SCIENTIFIC MANAGEMENT?

Scientific management (also called Taylorism)[4], was a theory of management that analyzed and synthesized workflows. Taylo developed, the core ideas of scientific management in the 1880s and 1890s in manuufacturing industies and were first published in his monographs [A Piece Rate System (1895), Shop Management (1903)][5] and ['The Principles of Scientific

---

[4] Mitcham, Carl and Adam, Briggle Management in Mitcham (2005) p.1153, quote: [Nevertheless, regardless of outcomes and the fact that the term has fallen out of use, "'scientific management,' as well as its near synonym, 'Taylorism,' have been absorbed into the living tissue of American life" (Kanigel 1997, p. 6)

[5] Taylor, Frederick Winslow (1903), Shop Management, New York, NY, USA: American Society of Mechanical Engineers, OCLC 2365572. 'Shop Management' began as an address by Taylor to a meeting of the ASME,

Management' (1911)].[6] Its main objective was improving economic efficiency, especially labor productivity. It was one of the earliest attempts to apply science to the engineering of processes and to management.

Taylor whilst working working as a lathe operator and foreman at Midvale Steel, noticed the natural differences in productivity between workers, which were driven by various causes, including: differences in talent; intelligence; or motivations. He was one of the first people to try to apply science to this application, i.e. understanding why and how these differences existed and how best practices could be analyzed and synthesized, then propagated to the other workers through standardization of process steps. He believed that decisions based upon tradition and rules of thumb should be replaced by precise procedures developed after careful study of an individual at work, including through time and motion studies, which would tend to discover or synthesize the "one best way" to do any given task,[7] with the goal and promise encompassing both an increase in productivity and reduction of effort.[8]

The peak of influence of scientific management came in the 1910s; by the 1920s it was, however, influential but had begun an era of competition,

---

which published it in pamphlet form. The link here takes the reader to a 1912 republication by Harper & Brothers.

[6] Taylor, Frederick Winslow (1911), The Principles of Scientific Management, New York, NY, USA and London, UK: Harper & Brothers, LCCN 11010339, OCLC 233134.

[7] IBID, pp 117-118

[8] Morf, Martin (1983), ' Eight Scenarios for Work in the Future', p.15.

syncretism and criticism, with opposing or complementary ideas in place. Although scientific management as school of thought or a distinct theory was obsolete by the 1930s, but nevertheless most of its themes remained and are still important parts of industrial engineering and management today.

These include: analysis; synthesis; logic; rationality; empiricism; work ethic; efficiency and elimination of waste; standardization of best practices; disdain for tradition preserved merely for its own sake or merely to protect the social status of particular workers with particular skill sets; the transformation of craft production into mass production; and knowledge transfer between workers and from workers into tools, processes, and documentation.

The scientific management's application was contingent on a high level of managerial control over employee work practices, that necessitated a higher ratio of managerial workers to laborers than previous management methods. The great difficulty in accurately differentiating any such intelligent, detail-oriented management from mere misguided micromanagement also caused interpersonal friction between workers and managers, and social tensions between the blue-collar and white-collar classes of workers.

Scientific management is a variation on the theme of economic efficiency; it is a late 19th and early 20th century instance of the larger recurring theme in human life of increasing efficiency, decreasing waste, and using empirical methods to decide what matters, rather than uncritically accepting pre-existing ideas of what matters. Thus it is a chapter in a larger narrative that includes many ideas and fields, from the folk wisdom of thrift to a profusion of applied-science successors, including: time and motion study; the Efficiency Movement (which was the broader cultural echo of scientific management's impact on business managers specifically); Fordism; operations management; operations research; industrial engineering; manufacturing engineering; logistics, business process management; business process reengineering, lean manufacturing, and Six Sigma.

The greatest use of the term "scientific management", in management literature today, is with reference to the work of Taylor and his disciples in contrast to newer, improved iterations of efficiency-seeking methods In political and sociological terms, Taylorism can be seen as the division of labor pushed to its logical extreme, with a consequent de-skilling of the worker and dehumanisation of the workers and the workplace. Taylorism along with Fordism, is often mentioned because it was closely associated with mass production methods in factories, which was its earliest application. Today, task-oriented optimization of work tasks is nearly omnipresent in industry. The theory behind it has evolved greatly since Taylor's day, is sometimes implemented poorly even now.

Taylor observed that some workers were more talented than others, and that even smart ones were often unmotivated. Taylor also observed that most workers who are forced to perform repetitive tasks tend to work at the slowest rate that goes unpunished. This slow rate of work has been observed in many industries in many countries[9] and has been called by various terms including: "soldiering";[10] (reflecting the way conscripts may approach following orders), "dogging it",[11] "goldbricking",[12] "hanging it out";[13] and "ca

---

[9] Taylor 1911, pp. 13–14.

[10] Merriam-Webster.com, "Soldier (intransitive verb", sense 2

[11] Merriam-Webster.com, "dog (transitive verb", below sense 2, related

canae".[14]

Managers may call it by those names or "loafing"[15] or "malingering"; workers may call it "getting through the day" or "preventing management from abusing us". Taylor used the term "soldiering" and observed that, when paid the same amount, workers will tend to do the amount of work that the slowest among them does.[16] This reflects the idea that workers have a vested interest in their own well-being, and do not benefit from working above the defined rate of work when it will not increase their remuneration. He therefore proposed that the work practice that had been developed in most work environments was crafted, intentionally or unintentionally, to be very inefficient in its execution. He posited that time and motion studies combined with rational analysis and synthesis could uncover one best method for performing any particular task, and that prevailing methods were seldom equal to these best methods.

Taylor rejected the notion, which was universal in his day and still prevalent even now, of the secret magic of the craftsman—that the trades, including manufacturing, were black arts that could not be analyzed and could only be performed by craft production methods. Crucially, Taylor himself prominently acknowledged that if each employee's compensation was linked to their output, their productivity would go up,[17] thereby his compensation plans usually included piece rates.

---

phrasal verb "dog it"
[12] Merriam-Webster.com, "goldbrick (verb)", intratrasitive sense.
[13] Taylor 1911, pp. 13–14.
[14] IBID
[15] Taylor 1911, pp. 19, 23, 82, 95.
[16] Taylor 1911, pp. 13–29, 95.
[17] Taylor 1911, pp. 13–29, 95.

Towards Understanding Management Principles and Process

Taylor's view of workers was complex,[18] having both insightful and obtuse elements. Anyone who manages a large team of workers sees from experience that Taylor was correct that some workers could not be relied upon for talent or intelligence; today enterprises still find that talent is a scarce resource. But he failed to leave room in his system for the workers who *did* have talent or intelligence. Some of them would be duly utilized during the early phases (the studying and designing), but what about smart workers in years afterwards who would start out among the ranks of the drones? What opportunities would they have for career advancement or socioeconomic advancement? He also failed to properly consider the fate of the drone-ish workers themselves. Maybe they did lack the ability for higher-level jobs, but what about keeping them satisfied or placated in their existing roles?

Taylor was so immersed in the vast work immediately in front of him (getting the world to understand and to implement scientific management's earliest phases) that he failed to strategize about the next steps (sustainability of the system after the early phases). Taylorism, however, took some steps toward addressing their needs (e.g., Taylor advocated frequent breaks and good pay),[19] but Taylor nevertheless had a condescending view of less intelligent workers, whom he sometimes compared to draft animals.[20]

Many other thinkers soon stepped forward to offer better ideas on the roles that humans would play in mature industrial systems, e.g. James Hartness, a

---

[18] Taylor 1911.

[19] Taylor 1911, pp. 13–29, 95.

[20] Taylor 1911, p. 59.

fellow ASME member, published 'The Human Factor in Works Management[21] in 1912; and Frank Gilbreth and Lillian Moller Gilbreth offered alternatives to Taylorism, whist the human relations school of management evolved in the 1930s.

Some scholars, such as Harry Braverman,[22] insisted that human relations did not replace Taylorism but rather that both approaches were complementary as Taylorism determining the actual organisation of the work process, whilst human relations helping to adapt the workers to the new procedures. Today's efficiency-seeking methods (such as lean manufacturing), include respect for workers and fulfillment of their needs as inherent parts of the theory. Clearly a syncretism has occurred since Taylor's day, although its implementation has been uneven, as lean management, in capable hands, has produced good results for both managers and workers, whilst in incompetent hands, has damaged enterprises.

Implementations of scientific management usually failed to account for several inherent challenges, such as: (a)individuals are different from each other: the most efficient way of working for one person may be inefficient for another; and (b) the economic interests of workers and management are rarely identical, so that both the measurement processes and the retraining required by Taylor's methods are frequently resented and sometimes sabotaged by the workforce.

---

[21] Hartness, James (1912), ' The human factor in works management', New York and London: McGraw-Hill. Republished by Hive Publishing Company as Hive management history series no. 46, ISBN 978-0-87960-047-1.

[22] Braverman, Harry (1998) [1974], Labor and Monopoly Capital: The Degradation of Work in the 20th Century', New York, NY, USA: Republication by Monthly Review Press, ISBN 0-85345-940-1.

In fact, Taylor himself recognized these challenges and had some good ideas for meeting them, but nevertheless, his own implementations of his system (e.g., Watertown Arsenal, Link-Belt corporation, Midvale, Bethlehem) were never really very successful. They plugged along rockily and eventually were overturned, usually after Taylor had left. And countless managers who later aped or worshiped Taylor did even worse jobs of implementation. Typically they were less analytically talented managers who had latched onto scientific management as the latest fad for cutting the unit cost of production.

Like bad managers even today, these were the people who used the big words without any deep understanding of what they meant. Taylor knew that scientific management could not work unless the workers benefited from the profit increases that it generated. Taylor had developed a method for generating the increases, for the dual purposes of owner/manager profit and worker profit, realizing that the methods relied on both of those results in order to work correctly, but many owners and managers seized upon the methods thinking (wrongly) that the profits could be reserved solely or mostly for themselves and the system could endure indefinitely merely through force of authority. But workers are necessarily human and they have personal needs and interpersonal friction. Also they face very real difficulties introduced when jobs become so efficient that they have no time to relax, and so rigid that they have no permission to innovate.

Scientific management was naturally appealing to managers of planned economies, because central economic planning relies on the idea that the expenses that go into economic production can be precisely predicted and can be optimized by design. The opposite theoretical pole would be an extremist variant of laissez-faire thinking in which the invisible hand of free markets is the only possible "designer". In reality most economies today are somewhere in between.

Scientific management was one of the first attempts to systematically treat management and process improvement as a scientific problem. It was probably the first to do so in a "bottom-up" way, which is a concept that remains useful even today, in concert with other concepts. Two corollaries of this primacy are that (a) scientific management became famous and (b) it was merely the first iteration of a long-developing way of thinking, and many iterations have come since. Nevertheless, common elements unite them. With the advancement of statistical methods, quality assurance (QA) and quality control (QC) could begin in the 1920s and 1930s.

During the 1940s and 1950s, the body of knowledge for doing scientific management evolved into operations management, operations research (OR), and management cybernetics. In the 1980s total quality management (TQM) became widely popular, and in the 1990s "re-engineering" went from a simple word to a mystique (a kind of evolution that, unfortunately, draws bad managers to jump on the bandwagon without understanding what the bandwagon is). Today's Six Sigma and lean manufacturing could be seen as new kinds of scientific management, although their evolutionary distance from the original is so great that the comparison might be misleading. In particular, Shigeo Shingo, one of the originators of the Toyota Production System, believed that this system and Japanese management culture in general should be seen as a kind of scientific management.

Peter Drucker saw Frederick Taylor as the creator of knowledge management, because the aim of scientific management was to produce knowledge about how to improve work processes. Although, the typical application of scientific management was manufacturing, Taylor himself advocated scientific management for all sorts of work, including the management of universities and government. For example, Taylor believed scientific management could be extended to "the work of salesmen". Shortly after his death, his acolyte Harlow S. Person began to lecture corporate audiences on the possibility of using Taylorism for "sales engineering"[23] [Person was talking about engineering the processes that salespeople use— not about sales engineering in the way that we use that term today]. This was a watershed insight in the history of corporate marketing.

Today's militaries employ all of the major goals and tactics of scientific management, if not under that name. Of the key points, all but wage incentives for increased output are used by modern military organizations. Wage incentives rather appear in the form of skill bonuses for enlistments. Scientific management has had an important influence in sports, where stop watches and motion studies rule the day.[24] Modern human resources can be seen to have begun in the scientific management era, most notably in the writings of Katherine M. H. Blackford, who was also a

---

[23] Dawson, Michael (2005), *The Consumer Trap: Big Business Marketing in American Life* (paper ed.), Urbana, IL, USA: University of Illinois Press, ISBN 0-252-07264-2.

[24] Taylor himself enjoyed sports, especially tennis and golf. He and a partner won a national championship in doubles tennis. He invented improved tennis racquets and improved golf clubs, although other players liked to tease him for his unorthodox designs, and they did not catch on as replacements for the mainstream implements.

proponent of eugenics.

7.3   SCIENTIFIC MANAGEMENT BY TAYLOR

Fredrick Winslow Taylor (March 20, 1856 - March 21, 1915) commonly known as 'Father of Scientific Management' started his career as an operator and rose to the position of chief engineer. He conducted various experiments during this process which forms the basis of scientific management. It implies application of scientific principles for studying & identifying management problems. In Taylors view, if a work is analysed scientifically it will be possible to find one best way to do it.

According to Taylor, "Scientific Management is an art of knowing exactly what you want your men to do and seeing that they do it in the best and cheapest way". Hence scientific management is a thoughtful, organized, and dual approach towards the job of management against Rule of Thumb or hit/ miss rule. According to Drucker, however, "The cost of scientific management is the organized study of work, the analysis of work into simplest element and then systematic management of worker's performance of each element".

7.4   FAYOL VS TAYLOR ON THE STUDY OF SCIENTIFIC MANAGEMENT

Both Fayol anf Taylor have contributed to development of science of management. The contribution of these two pioneers in the field of science of management has been reviewed as "The work of Taylor and Fayol was, of course, especially complementary. They both realized that problem of personnel & its management at all levels is the key to individual success. Both applied scientific method to this problem that Taylor worked primarily from operative level, from bottom to upward, while Fayol concentrated on managing director and work downwards, was merely a reflection of their very different careers".

Likewise, both emphasized mutual co-operation between employment and employees. But Fayol's theory is more widely applicable than that of Taylor, although Taylor's philosophy has undergone a big change Under influence of modern development, but Fayol's principles of management have stood the test of time and are still being accepted as the core of management theory.

According to Psychologists, Taylor's study had following drawbacks: -

- ➢ Ignores human factors - Considers them as machines. Ignores human requirements, want and aspirations.
- ➢ Separation of Planning and Doing.
- ➢ Dissatisfaction - Comparing performance with others.
- ➢ No best way - Scientific management does not give one best way for solving problems.
- ➢ Both, Fayol and Taylor, however, differ from each other in following aspects: -
- ➢ Taylor looked at management from supervisory viewpoint & tried to improve efficiency at operating level. He moved upwards while formulating theory. On the other hand, Fayol analyzed management from level of top management downward. Thus, Fayol could afford a broader vision than Taylor.
- ➢ Taylor focused his attention on fact by management and his principles are applicable on shop floor. But Fayol concentrated on function of

managers and on general principles of management wheel could be equally applied in all.

➤ Main aim of Taylor - to improve labor productivity & to eliminate all type of waste through standardization of work & tools. Fayol attempted to develop a universal theory of management and stressed upon need for teaching the theory of management.

➤ Taylor called his philosophy "Scientific Management" while Fayol described his approach as "A general theory of administration".

The comparison of fayol and and Taloy on differet basis is shown in Fig. 2h.

BASES	FAYOL	TAYLOR
Scope of principles	These are applicable in all kinds of organization regarding their management affairs	These principles are restricted to production activities
Human Aspect	Fayol pays due regards on human element, e.g. Principle of initiative, Espirit De' Corps and Equity recognizes a need for human relations	Scientific management
Efficiency & administration	Stressed on general administration	Stressed on efficiency
Status	Father of management principles	Father of scientific management
Approach	It has macro-approach and discuses general principles of management which are applicable in every field of management.	It has micro-approach because it is restricted to factory only
Achievement	Administrative management	Scientific management

Fig. 2h

7.5   PRINCIPLES OF SCIENTIFIC MANAGEMENT

Rrinciple 1: Development of Science for each part of men's job (replacement of rule of thumb

The main feature of this principle include but nolt limited to: (a) this means replacement of odd rule of thumb by the use of method of enquiry, investigation, data collection, analysis and framing of rules; (b) this principle suggests that work assigned to any employee should be observed, analyzed with respect to each and every element and part and time involved in it; and under scientific management, decisions are made on the basis of facts and by the application of scientific decisions.

Rrinciple 2: Scientific Selection, Training and Development of Workers

There should be scientifically designed procedure for the selection of workers encompassing: (a) physical, mental and other requirement should be specified for each and every job; (b) workers should be selected and trained to make them fit for the job; (c) the management has to provide opportunities for development of workers having better capabilities; and according to Taylor efforts should be made to develop each employee to his/her greatest level and efficiency and prosperity.

Rrinciple 3: Co-operation between Management & workers or Harmony not discord

The main feature of this principle include but nolt limited to: (a) There should be no conflict between managers and workers as it is only through co-operation that the goals of the enterprise can be achieved efficiently; (b) Taylor believed in co-operation and not individualism the interest of employer and employees should be fully harmonized so as to secure mutually understanding relations between them.

Rrinciple 4: Division of Responsibility

The main feature of this principle include but nolt limited to: (a) this principle determines the concrete nature of roles to be played by different level of managers and workers; (b)the management should assume the responsibility of planning the work whereas workers should be concerned with execution of task; and planning is to be separated from execution.

Rrinciple 5: Maximum Prosperity for Employer & Employees

The main feature of this principle include but nolt limited to (a) the aim of scientific management is to see maximum prosperity for employer and employees; (b)It is important only when there is opportunity for each worker to attain his highest efficiency; (c) there should be maximum output in place of restricted output; (d) both managers and workers should be paid handsomely; and (e)Maximum output and optimum utilization of resources will bring higher profits for the employer and better wages for the workers.

Rrinciple 6: Mental Revolution

The main feature of this principle include but nolt limited to: (a) the workers and managers should have a complete change of outlook towards their mutual relation and work effort; (b) the worker shold be disciplined, sincere, and loyal in fulfilling the task assigned to them; (c) it requires that management should create suitable working condition and solve all problems scientifically; (d) likewise workers should attend their jobs with utmost attention, devotion and carefulness. They should not waste the resources of enterprise: (e) attractive remuneration should be provided to workers to boost up their moral and it would create a sense of belongingness among worker; and (f) there should be more production and economical growth at a faster rate.

7.6 TOOLS AND TECHNIQUES OF SCIENTIFIC MANAGEMENT

There are various tools of scientific management, such as: Time Study; Motion Study; Differential Piece Wage Plan; Fucntional Foremanship; Standardization; and Other Techniques.

7.6.1 Time Study

The features of this tool include but not limited to the following:

➢ It is a technique which enables the manager to ascertain standard time taken for performing a specified job.
➢ This technique is based on the study of an average worker having reasonable skill and ability.
➢ Every job or every part of it is studied in detail.
➢ Taylor maintained that Fair day's work should be determined through observations, experiment and analysis by keeping in view an average worker's eqation: **Standard Time × Working Hours = Fair Day's Work .**
➢ Average worker is selected and assigned the job and then with the help of a stop watch, time is ascertained for performing that particular job.

7.6.2 Motion Study

The features of this tool include but not limited to the following:

➢ By undertaking motion study an attempt is made to know whether some elements of a job can be eliminated combined or their sequence can be changed to achieve necessary rhythm.

➢ The purpose of motion study is to eliminate useless motions and determine the bet way of doing the job.
➢ In this study, movement of body and limbs required to perform a job are closely observed, i.e. it refers to the study of movement of an operator on machine involved in a particular task.
➢ Motion study increases the efficiency and productivity of workers by cutting down all wasteful motions.

7.6.3 Differential Piece Wage Plan

The features of this tecnique include but not limited to the following:

➢ This system is a source of incentive to workers who improving their efficiency in order to get more wages.
➢ This technique of wage payment is based on efficiency of worker.
➢ The efficient workers are paid more wages than inefficient one, i.e. those workers who produce less than standard number of pieces are paid wages at lower rate than prevailing rate.
➢ It encourages inefficient workers to improve their performance and achieve their standards.
➢ It leads to mass production which minimizes cost and maximizes profits.

7.6.5 Functional Foremanship

The features of this tecnique include but not limited to the following:

➢ This technique was developed to improve the quality of work as single supervisor may not be an expert in all the aspects of the work, therefore workers are to be supervised by specialist foreman.

➤ Taylor advocated functional foremanship for achieving ultimate specification.

➤ The scheme of functional foremanship is an extension of principle pf specialization at the supervisory level.

➤ Taylor also advocated appointment of 8 foramen, 4 at the planning level and other 4 at implementation level. The model is shown in Fig. 1.2i.

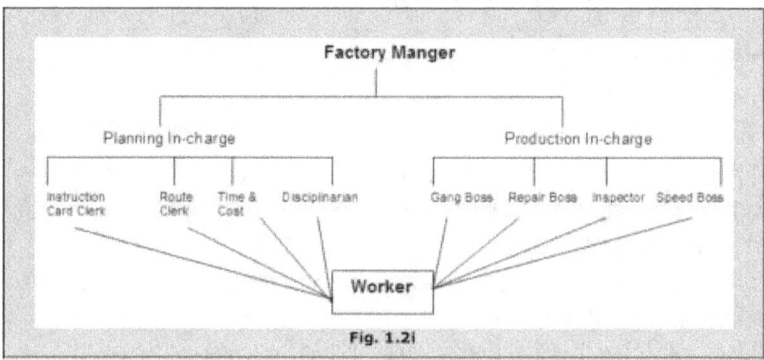

Fig. 1.2i

The names and function of these specialist foremen are:

➤ Inspector is concerned with maintaining the quality of product.

➤ Instruction card clerk concerned with tagging down of instructions according to which workers are required to perform their job

➤ Time and cost clerk is concerned with setting a time table for doing a job and specifying the material and labor cost involved in it.

➤ Route clerk determines the route through which raw materials has to be passed.

➢ Shop Disciplinarians are concerned with making rules and regulations to ensure discipline in the organization.
➢ Gang boss makes the arrangement of workers, machines, tools, workers etc.
➢ Speed boss concerned with maintaining the speed and to remove delays in the production process.
➢ Repair boss concerned with maintenance of machine, tools and equipments.

7.6.6 Standardization

The features of this tecnique include but not limited to the following:
➢ Standardization is a means of achieving economics of production.
➢ Standardization implies the physical attitude of products should be such that it meets the requirements and needs of customers.
➢ Taylor advocated that tools and equipments as well as working conditions should be standardized to achieve standard output from workers.
➢ Standardization seems to ensure: (a) the line of product is restricted to predetermined type, form, design, size, weight, quality, etc.; (b) there is manufacture of identical parts and components; (c) quality and standards have been maintained; and (d) standard of performance are established for workers at all levels.

7.6.7 Other Tools and Techniques

Various other techniques have been developed to create ordeal relationship between management and workers and also to create better understanding on part of works. Such tools and techniques include: use of instruction cards; strict rules and regulations; graphs; slides;and charts etc. so as to increase efficiency of workers and increase productivity.

7.7   CRITICISM OF SCIENTIFIC MANAGEMENT

Although the scientific management is accepted that it enables the management to put resources to its best possible use and manner, but nevertheless it met many criticism, such as shown in Fig. 1.2j.

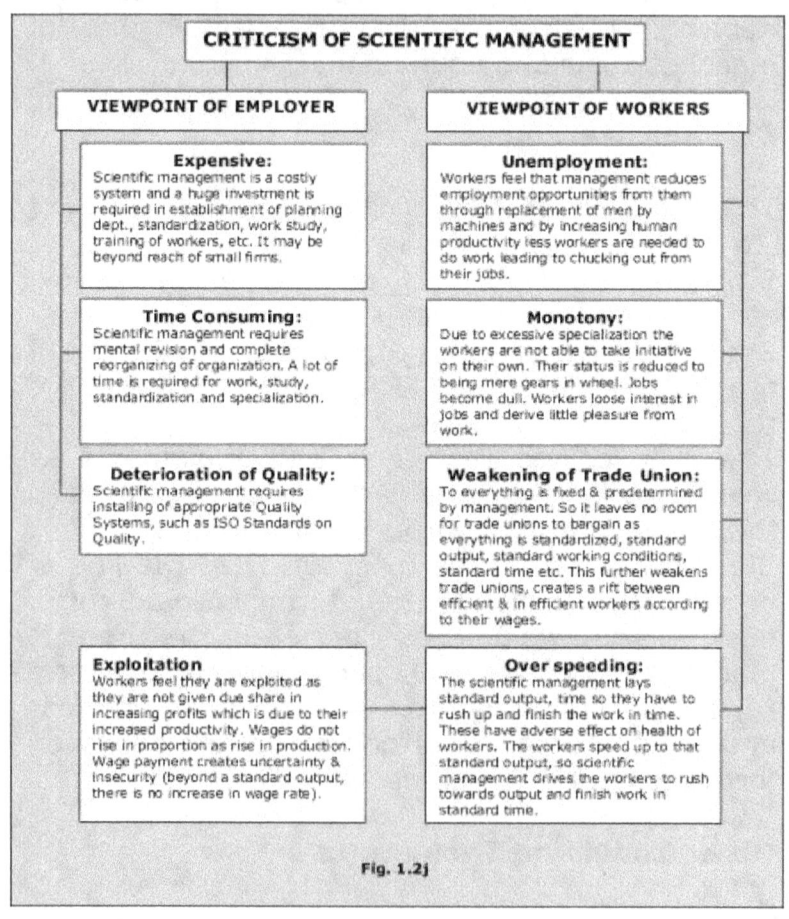

Fig. 1.2j

Chapter 8

THE MANAGEMENT PROCESS: THE FUCTIONS OF MANAGEMENT

8.1 INTRODUUCTION

As we have aleady discussed, management has been described as a social process involving responsibility for economical and effective planning and regulation of operation of an enterprise in the fulfillment of given purposes. It is the process of working through individuals and groups to accomplish organizational goals and objectives. It is a dynamic process consisting of various elements and activities, where these activities are different from operative functions like marketing, finance, purchase etc. Rather these activities are those which are common to each and every manger irrespective of his level or status. The management process, by and large, consists of four primary functions, namely: planning, organizing, leading/ motivating/directing, and controlling. A model for Management Process is aleady shown in Fig. 1.1.

Differen experts have classified differently functions of management. According to *George & Jerry*, "There are four fundamental functions of management i.e. planning, organizing, actuating and controlling". According to Henry Fayol, "To manage is to forecast and plan, to organize, to command, & to control". Whereas Luther Gullick has given a keyword 'POSDCORB' where P stands for Planning, O for Organizing, S for Staffing, D for Directing, Co for Co-ordination, R for reporting , and B for Budgeting. The most widely accepted fnctions are: Planning, Organizing, Staffing, Directing and Controlling as given by KOONTZ and O'DONNEL, see Fig. 1.2k.

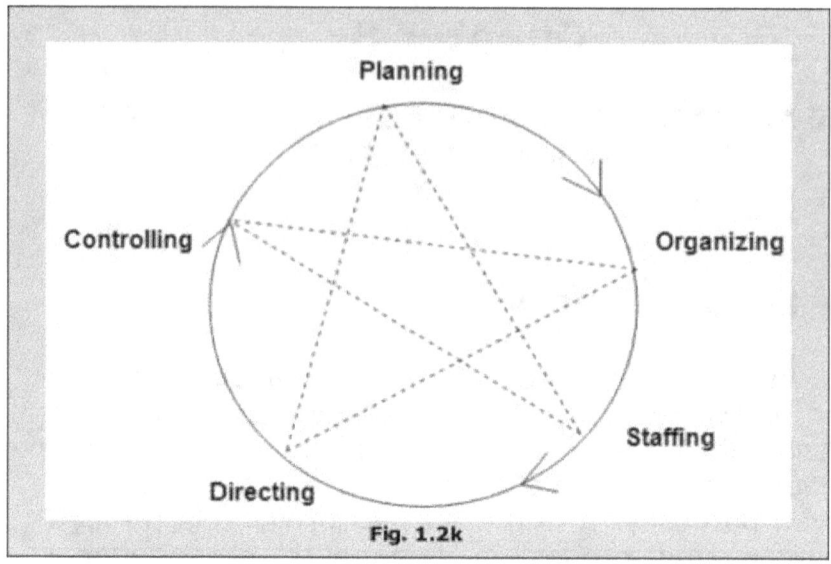

Fig. 1.2k

For theoretical purposes, it may be convenient to separate the function of management but practically these functions are overlapping in nature i.e. they are highly inseparable as each function blends into the other and each affects the performance of others

8.2   PLANNING FUNCTION OF MANAGEMENT

It is the basic function of management as it deals with chalking out a future course of action and deciding in advance the most appropriate course of actions for achievement of pre-determined goals. According to KOONTZ, "Planning is deciding in advance - what to do, when to do & how to do. It bridges the gap from where we are and where we want to be". A plan is a future course of actions. It is an exercise in problem solving and decision making. Planning is determination of courses of action to achieve desired goals. Thus, planning is a systematic thinking about ways & means for accomplishment of pre-determined goals. Planning is necessary to ensure proper utilization of human and non-human resources. It is all pervasive, it is an intellectual activity and it also helps in avoiding confusion, uncertainties, risks, wastages etc.

In its simplest form planning is the thinking that precedes doing. It means determining an organization's goals/ objectives and preparing plans and schedules to achieve them. Decision making (a part of planning process) involves selecting a course of action from a set of alternatives. Therefore, planning and decision making combined is task of determining courses of action to achieve the desired goals.

Planning and decision making help maintain management effectiveness by serving as guides for future activities. Knowing where the manager wants his organization to be at a given time in the future, the manager develops a strategy for getting there. This development process is called strategic planning. Important elements in planning include but not limited to the following:

➢ Identifying and interpreting goals and objectives passed down from higher level of management.
➢ Collating the ideas/thoughts of the employees directly involved in the work activities.
➢ Formulating policies and procedures to accomplish the desired goals and objectives and making recommendation for their implementation.
➢ Appraising alternatives and selecting suitable activities and programs that will lead to successful results.
➢ Preparing schedules and establishing completion targets.
➢ Determining performance and progress monitoring standards.
➢ Identify resources to accomplish the assigned tasks.

8.3   ORGANIZING FUNCTION OF MANAGEMENT

Organization is the next phase of management process. It is the process of bringing together: physical; financial; and human resources and developing productive relationship amongst them for achievement of organizational goals. According to Henry Fayol: "To organize a business is to provide it with everything useful or its functioning i.e. raw material, tools, capital and personnel". To organize a business involves determining and providing human and non-human resources to the organizational structure.   After workable plan is developed through the process of planning and decision making, the next step is to organize the manpower and other resources including capital, equipment, raw materials, facilities, etc. to carry out the plan in the most productive way. Important elements in organizing include but not limited to the following:

> ➢ Identification of activities.
> ➢ Assessing availability of sufficient manpower and adequate staffing to accomplish the goals and objectives.
> ➢ Classification of grouping of activities.
> ➢ Delineating responsibility and authority at all levels of the organization.
> ➢ Designing organization and its structure i.e. aligning of major functions and structuring into effective work units/teams by considering both line as well as staff functions etc., and formulating organization charts.
> ➢ Assignment of duties and preparing job description.
> ➢ Preparing manuals and administrative guidelines to communicate at all levels, how responsibility

and authority has been delineated. Delegation of authority and creation of responsibility.

➢ Preparing a communication system for reporting.
➢ Formulating methods and procedures for problem solving and resolution of conflicts.
➢ Organizing facilities and equipment needed to accomplish assigned tasks.
➢ Coordinating authority and responsibility relationships.

8.4   STAFFING FUNCTION OF MANAGEMENY

Staffing has assumed greater importance in the recent years due to advancement of technology, increase in size of business, complexity of human behavior etc. It is the function of manning the organization structure and keeping it manned. The main purpose of staffing is to put right man on right job i.e. square pegs in square holes and round pegs in round holes. According to Kootz & O'Donell, "Managerial function of staffing involves manning the organization structure through proper and effective selection process, appraisal and development of personnel to fill the roles designed un the structure". Staffing involves:

➢ Manpower Planning (estimating man power in terms of searching, choose the person and giving the right place).
➢ Recruitment, selection & placement.
➢ Training & development.
➢ Remuneration.
➢ Performance appraisal.
➢ Promotions & transfer.

8.7   LEADING/DIRECTING FUNCTION OF MANAGEMENT

It is that part of managerial function which actuates the organizational methods to work efficiently for achievement of organizational purposes. It is considered life-spark of the enterprise which sets it in motion the action of people because planning, organizing and staffing are the mere preparations for doing the work. Direction is that inert-personnel aspect of management which deals directly with influencing, guiding, supervising, motivating sub-ordinate for the achievement of organizational goals. Direction has following elements: Supervision; Motivation; Leadership; and Communication

Supervision: implies overseeing the work of subordinates by their superiors. It is the act of watching & directing work & workers.

Motivation: means inspiring, stimulating or encouraging the sub-ordinates with zeal to work. Positive, negative, monetary, non-monetary incentives may be used for this purpose.

Leadership: may be defined as a process by which manager guides and influences the work of subordinates in desired direction.

Communications: is the process of passing information, experience, opinion etc from one person to another. It is a bridge of understanding.

This is the next phase of management after organizing. It is not enough to put people into various slots and expect that everything will take care of itself. Leading/ is most important and perhaps the hardest part of management process. Leading is the set of process used to get members of the organization to work together as a team to further the interest of the organization. Important elements in leading/directing include but not limited to the following:

> Motivating employees to expand efforts. This element includes recognizing employees contribution, delegating authority to make decisions, and creating an environment in which employees can also meet their needs whilst meeting the needs of their organization.
> Instituting participative management and management by objectives, if appropriate.
> Applying appropriate leadership style which focuses on what the manager does to encourage organizational performance.
> Effectively dealing with group and group processes.
> Instituting effective communication.
> Instituting training and human resources development to achieve higher level of motivation resulting in improved performance.

8.6   CONTROLLING FUNCTION OF MANAGEMENT

Controlling is the final phase of management process and involves monitoring progress and evaluating activities by setting standards and checklists for evaluating work against these standards, sampling the work flow, and collecting feedback, etc.

Controlling implies measurement of accomplishment against the standards and correction of deviation if any to ensure achievement of organizational goals. The purpose of controlling is to ensure that everything occurs in conformities with the standards. An efficient system of control helps to predict deviations before they actually occur. According to *Theo Haimann*, "Controlling is the process of checking whether or not proper progress is being made towards the objectives and goals and acting if necessary, to correct any deviation". According to Koontz & O'Donell, "Controlling is the measurement and correction of performance activities of subordinates in order to make sure that the enterprise objectives and plans desired to obtain them as being accomplished".

Controlling helps to ensure the effectiveness and efficiency needed for successful management. Important elements in controlling include but not limited to the following:

➢ Formulating ways and means to assess whether goals, objectives, or standards have been met in a timely and cost effective manner.
➢ Establishing of standard performance.
➢ Devising methods and procedures by which the use of the various resources can be measured and evaluated.
➢ Performaning measurement of actual performance.
➢ Establishing feedback systems to monitor main milestones as the work progresses.
➢ Making comparison of actual performance with the standards and finding out deviation if any.
➢ Taking vorrective action.
➢ Reporting the status of work and/or project activities to the management.

Chapter 9

MANAGEMENT THEORIES BRIEFLY EXPLAINED

9.1 CLASSICAL MANAGEMENT THEORY

There are three major schools of management thought: classical, behavioral, and quantitative. Classical management theory includes two different approaches to management: i.e., scientific management and classical organization theory. Scientific management which is generally concerned with the management of work and workers developed from the pioneering research of five scholars, namely Frederic W. Taylor (1856-1915), Henry Gantt (1861-1919), Harrington Emerson (1853-1931), Frank Gilbreth (1868-1924), and Lillian Gilbreth (1878-1972). However Taylor played the dominant role.

Taylor was very much interested in developing solutions to the problem of labour efficiency. Taylor approach can be summarized as follows:

Firstly develop a science for each element of man's work, secondly select and then train, teach, and develop the workman, thirdly co-operate with the workers to insure that all the work being done is in accordance with the principles of the science which has been developed; fourthly provide equal division of the work and responsibility between the management and workmen. Analyse the work situation (job to be done, work force, and a manager), carry out task analysis (work breakdown structure and resources allocation, etc.), and then match tasks with the worker and finally provide continued management.

Towards Understanding Management Principles and Process

Frank and Lillian Gilbreth were a husband-wife team of industrial engineers who developed numerous techniques and strategies for eliminating inefficiency. They were primarily interested in time-and-motion study and job specifications.

Henry Gantt developed two specific techniques for improving worker output. First he developed the Gantt Chart which is a means of Scheduling Work and his second major contribution was to deal with Pay Systems (minimum wage, bonus, reward for the supervisors, etc.).

Harrington Emerson was a strong advocator of making a strict distinction between line and staff roles in organizations.

Whereas scientific management deals with the jobs of individual employees, classical organizational theory focuses on managing the whole organization. Key contributors to classical organizational theory included Henri Fayol (1841-1925), Lyndall Urwick (1891-1983), Max Weber (1864-1920), and Chester Bernard (1886-1961). Henri Fayol, drawing on over fifty years of his managerial experience, attempted to systematize the practice of management to provide guidance and directions to other managers. Part of his thinking was expressed in fourteen principles (Guidelines) for effective management (Fig. 1.2 refers).

Fayol was the first to identify the specific managerial functions mentioned above, i.e. planning, organizing, leading and controlling. Lyndall Urwick tried to synthesize and integrate scientific management with the work of Fayol and other classical organizational theorists and further advanced modern thinking about the management functions of planning, organizing and controlling.

Max Weber work on bureaucracy (the concept of which is based on a rational set of guidelines for structuring the organizations in the most efficient manner) laid the foundation for contemporary organizational theory.

Chester Bernard made significant contributions to management in his classic book 'The Functions of Executive'. He proposed a well known theory about the acceptance of authority.

9.2   BEHAVIORUAL MANAGEMENT THEORY

Behavioural Management Theory placed much more emphasis on individual attitude and behaviours and on group processes.   Behaviour management theory, characterized by a concern for individual and group behaviour, had its roots in the industrial psychology; but it emerged primarily as a result of the Hawthorn studies which involved manipulating illumination for one group of workers and comparing subsequent productivity in that group with productivity in another group whose illumination was not changed. The human relations movement assumed that improved employee satisfaction will lead to improved performance.

However, in practice this assumption is proved to be wrong. For the contemporary management point of view, organizational behaviour which is an outgrowth of behavioural management theory, is an important aspect. This field includes job satisfaction, stress, motivation, leadership, group dynamics, communication, organizational structure & design and interpersonal conflict, etc.

9.3 QUANTITATIVE MANAGEMENT THEORY

Quantitative Management Theory essentially applies quantitative techniques to problem solving and decision making. It has three components, namely management science, operation management and management information systems. The management science approach focuses specifically on the development of mathematical models. Operations management is somewhat less mathematical and techniques used include network modelling, queuing theory, break-even analysis, and simulation, etc. Management Information Systems (MIS) is a system designed to provide managers with the information theory needed to make informal decisions. A fully developed MIS contains data and related information about the organization itself and about its external environment.

The three schools of management thoughts, namely the classical, behavioural and quantitative are not competing or mutually exclusive but complement each other. The most important aspect of management approach is understanding and appreciation of the basic tenets of all these three schools and how to use them effectively.

9.4 INTEGRATING PERSPECTIVES FOR MANAGEMENT

Contingency theory, essentially, suggests that appropriate management behaviour in a given situation depends on (or is contingent on) a wide variety of elements (contingencies) and unlike the classical, behavioural, and quantitative schools, holds that universal solutions and principles cannot be applied to social systems such as organizations.

However, systems theory together with contingency perspectives can help integrate the three schools and consequently lead to effective management.

Among contemporary management perspectives, theory 'Z', as expounded by William Ouchi in 1981, is an attempt to integrate common business practices in the Type 'A' (American) organization and Type 'J' (Japanese) organization. It is expected that theory 'Z' management will become increasingly popular in the future. Excellence in Management is another recent popular approach to management theory, although such approaches have both positive and negative characteristics.

There are two relative new additions to management theory, the systems theory and contingency theory, which appear to have great potential for both as approaches to management and frameworks for integrating the classical, behavioural, and quantitative theories. A system in this context can be defined as an interrelated set of elements functioning as a whole. An organizational system unit consists of an equation such as shown in Fig. 1.3.

Here the inputs enter the system from the environment and then through technological and management process & transformation convert into outputs and provide a feedback to the system (after the environment reaction to these outputs).

Other contemporary management perspectives include concepts of managing the culture of a corporation, enhancing teamwork at the middle-management level, and selecting good companies to work for (from the viewpoint of the employee). The manager needs to draw from the variety of sources and perspective when making a decision on how to proceed with the tasks ahead.

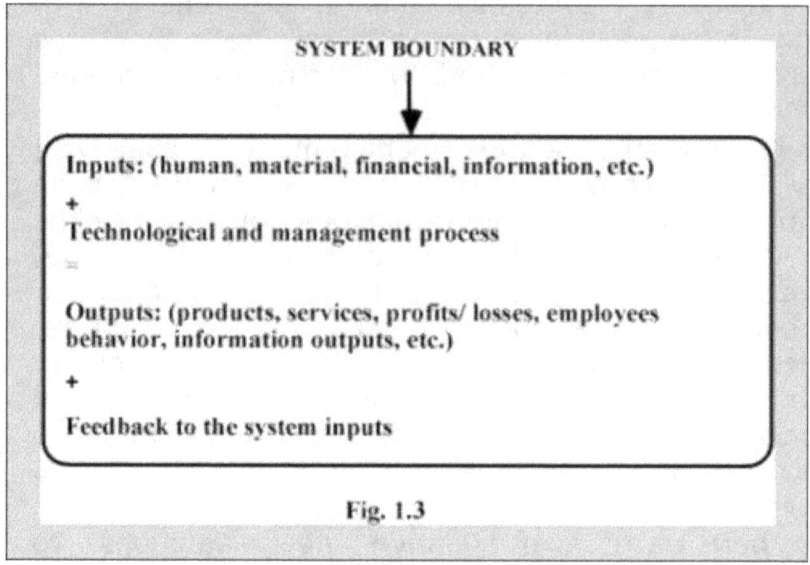

Fig. 1.3

Chapter 10

ROLES AND SKILLS OF MANAGERS

There are different managerial roles and different skills are needed to carry out these roles. The managerial roles may be numerous, but generally these fall into three basic categories, viz., interpersonal, informational and decisional. The interpersonal roles in turn may include figurehead, leader & liaison roles. Informational roles may include monitor, disseminator and spokesman roles. Decisional roles may include entrepreneur, disturbance handler, resource allocator and negotiator roles.

Managerial skills may be numerous, but key skills commonly described include technical skills, interpersonal skills, conceptual skills and also diagnostic skills and analytic skills. Technical skills are the skills necessary to accomplish specialized activities and effective task performance. Interpersonal skills include ability to communicate with, understand and motivate both individuals and groups within the organization. Conceptual skills depend on the manager's ability to think in the abstract; and enable the manager to understand that the objective should not be simply to minimize costs or maximize productivity, but to maximize profitability by optimizing the costs and productivity.

Diagnostic skills are also needed for managers to enable him to diagnose a problem in the organization by studying its symptoms. Analytical skills which provide ability in the manager to identify the key variables in a job setting, to see how these variables are inter-related and to decide which ones should receive the most attention. Analytic skills complement the diagnostic skills and in a sense are similar to conceptual skills. Diagnostic skills, in short, enable managers to understand a situation, whereas analytic skills enable managers to determine what to do in the situation and arrive at the recommendation.

Management skills may be acquired through education (formal course work and continuing education) or previous experience including training programmes or both. However, increasingly, successful managers are drawing on both experience and education as a means of acquiring and developing the skill they need.

Note: For further detail on the roles and skill of manager please refer to the companion book 3 entitled: "Managerial Skills and Competencies" of the 'In Search of Management Series.

Chapter 11

THE NATURE OF ORGANIZATIONAL ENVIRONMENT

The environment is the set of forces and conditions that surround and permeate an organization. There are three kinds of organizational environment i.e., general, task, and internal. An organization's general environment consists of those nonspecific elements i.e., the economic, technological, socio-cultural, political-legal and international, of the organization's surroundings that might affect the activities of that organization. The task environment consists of specific elements (i.e. competitors, customers, suppliers, regulators, unions and associates) of the organization's surroundings that are very likely to influence the organization.

The internal environment of an organization (also known as its climate or culture) is the perceptions that the members of an organization share regarding the organization's nature, norm, style and character. Since the environment of an organization is such a critical factor in its success, therefore, the managers should understand how the organization and the environment influence one another at various levels. Positions in an organization that involves linking two or more systems in different organizations are called boundary roles and individuals who occupy boundary roles are called boundary spanners.

BOUNDARY-SPANNERS PROCESS

Boundary spanners perform six basic functions i.e. representing the organization to the environment;

monitoring the environment for information that may be of value to the organization; trying to protect the organization from threats from the environment; serving as information processors; serving as negotiating agents (for acquiring inputs and disposing of outputs); and linking organizations and co-ordinate activities among them. Boundary spanners positions need to be filled by persons having right combination of personality, experience and skill.

SOCIAL RESPONSIBILITY

The organization carries also social responsibility i.e. obligation towards taking necessary actions that protect and improve the welfare of society as a whole, along with advancing its own interest. Socially responsible behaviour by managers is usually a matter of ethics and withstanding social pressures. Ethical behaviour should not be confused with the legal behaviour. Legal behaviour is that which is not prohibited by laws and regulation, whereas ethical behaviour is more subjective and may go beyond mere legality. Unethical behaviours include political bribes and gifts, improper reporting procedures, and violation of privacy.

Note: For further detail on the roles and skill of manager please refer to the comanion book 9 entitled: "Fundamentals Of Organiszation Structure And Design" and book 10 entitled: "Fundamentals Of Organization Planning And Development" of the 'In Search of Management Series'.

Chapter 12

ISLAMIC PERSPECTIVES ON MANAGEMENT AND ADMINISTRATION

There is an Islamic perspective to management. In Islam, believers are to conform to the teachings of the Quran and the Sunnah of Prophet Muhammad (SAW). Among Allah's creation, Man is the best and elevated to the rank of Allah's khalifah (vicegerent) on the Earth. As a khalifah, the Man has responsibilty to prosper the earth one lives on, thereby never stops striving to improve oneself and one's community. The Quran exhorts believers to continuously enjoin good and forbid evil, wheras Prophet Mhammad (SAW) has been depicted as possessing the attribute of altruism, meaning "sincerest concern for the well-being of others", embracing the attitude and practice of caring, sharing, nurturing and bonding in one's relationship with others.

It connotes: unselfish orientation towards the welfare of people; mindful of the feelings and needs of those around us; and always striving for win-win situations in life. In its socio-economic context, it is the antithesis of absolute capitalism, one-upmanship, survival of the fittest, and manipulation of others. The world today is so corruptible, gullible and materialistic that many nations and corporations operate without a soul or conscience mindedness. By and large, the capitalistic bottom-line of maximising profits has become the benchmark for purported success, pervading local, regional, national, and international organisational levels. Therefore, there is a dire need for management paradigm that transcends narrow chauvinism, neo-conservatism and jingoism – with a universal, egalitarian and magnanimous approach.This managerial approach is still regarded as a pragmatic model that can be used to get things done efficaciously.

For example, Theodore Levitt of Harvard described management as "the rational assessment of a situation and the systematic selection of goals and purposes (what is to be done?); the systematic development of strategies to achieve these goals; the marshalling of the required resources; the rational design, organisation, direction, and control of the activities required to attain the selected purposes; and finally, the motivating and rewarding of people to do the work." Michael Hart's *The 100: A ranking of the Most Influential Persons in History* (1978), mentions the uniqueness of Prophet Muhammad's leadership, placing the Prophet as the most influential leader in human history, whilst presenting the qualities of a leader who was a successful businessman, a spiritual reformer, a charismatic commander, a just administrator, a peace negotiator, a political strategist, a jurist, a wise counsellor, and a prescient statesman in his lifetime.

As in the days of Prophet Muhammad (SAW), modern management needs strong leadership and excellent organisational capabilities to achieve exponential success. The super-ordinate paradigm of leadership provided by Prophet Muhammad (SAW) can be explained by a three-dimensional orientation, fusing alignment, attunement and empowerment in organisational development. When these three dimensions are cast, the outcome will be organisational synergy, the framework within which the strategic altruistic mindset should operate and the future can be positively mapped.

Such an alignment constitutes an organisation's vision of greatness. It is the direction-setting aspect of leadership, the inductive process (as opposed to the conventional deductive process) that formulates vision and mission statements. It describes the business, the technology it envelopes, the methodology it pursues, and the culture it embraces. Alignment implies that everyone in the organisation is moving towards the same objective, each in agreement with the other. Where adjustments have to be made, the parties involved will sit in mutual consultation to resolve issues.

In Prophet Muhammad's leadership paradigm, alignment is synonymous with tawheed (the Oneness of God), which is tempered by iman (belief) and *taqwa* (God-fearing). If people within an organisation is God-conscious, have strong faith and adhere to a firm set of values, then the stage is set for greatness in every field. Attunement is the esprit de corps, the will, the emotions, the passion and the compassion that fires the process towards goal attainment. Attunement has to move in tandem with alignment.

In Prophet Muhammad's leadership model, attunement means ibadah – righteous deeds performed daily as acts of faith. When employees of an organisation continuously perform good deeds and shun bad behaviour, the environment becomes harmonious, thereby achieving best results. There is a tendency to be committed, truthful and loyal because they continuously perform acts of quality in daily work. Empowerment is the willingness to allow skilled and knowledgeable people to use their talents and energies at work. Quite often, organisations and even nations falter in the face of stiff competition or when adjusting to new technology because leaders are not confident in the abilities of their people. Such people feel de-motivated. But when alignment, attunement and empowerment are employed in strategic human resource development, people perform because they feel wanted and appreciated.

When management accords employees the right to share the organisational vision and mission, a purposeful sense of direction is communicated to all levels. Responsibility and authority get delegated; and as long as people's responses are consistent with the vision and mission statements, conflict will not arise because everyone would be gunning for the same target. Empowerment ensures down-liners are allowed the initiative and freedom to realise their full potential by planning, organising and controlling their activities for the good of their organisation, whilst synergy is derived from the old Greek word *synergein*, which means working together with heart and soul. Synergism is the result of simultaneous actions of separate agencies, creating a greater total effect than the sum of their individual efforts. Synergy is the extraordinary outcome of aligned, attuned and empowered people with shared values in action. It is the energy that flows through a team of people, producing greater performance.

In Prophet Muhammad's governance model, synergy implies movement towards al-falah (the forces of success and prosperity). Attunement, coupled with empowerment, involves consultation, motivation and building esprit de corps among team members, thereby involving the emotions, the intellect and commitment from the heart (istiqamah). When Prophet Muhammad (SAW) involved his players actively in the process of problem-solving and decision-making, everyone was enlightened about the opportunities, hardships, and dangers involved in the many campaigns against the enemy. Morale-wise, when decisions were made by mutual consultation or consensus, they not only increased the speed and efficiency of actual operations but also fostered a high degree of trust and support in the followers, providing them with a raison d'etre for their ongoing military expeditions. Every member becomes totally committed to the cause.

Chapter 13

SUMMARY AND CONCLUSION

Management, managers and organizations play a significant contribution to our daily activities. Therefore, it is important to clearly understand the main theme surrounding the management process. Management can be defined as the process of planning, organizing, leading and controlling an organization's human, material, financial and information resources to achieve organizational goals in an effective and efficient manner, whereas a manager is a person whose primary activities are a part of the management process.

Management function is more of a thinking in nature designed to implement a team's best effort whilst leadership is more of an influencing function designed to motivate a group to put forth its best efforts. Accordingly a manager's behaviour initiates: instructing others, organizing work flow, planning/ goal setting for the team, supporting/ coaching subordinates, problem solving, co-ordination, etc. On the other hand a leader's behaviour exhibits a mentor for others, establishing a work culture, acting as a resource, creating opportunities for growths, challenging others, and setting an overall vision, etc. In other words the leadership function tends to focus more on task issues. However, in today's dramatically changing competitive landscape and in response to the way modern organizations are now tending to perform i.e. restructuring their operations by laying off people, and reinventing their systems by re-engineering, etc, both functions are equally required to achieve excellence and success.

The trend in modern Leadership is to adapt to people, rather than fit people into an existing model, by creating an organizational framework in which people can react quickly and remain flexible. Instead of treating people as replaceable parts in a grand mechanized bureaucracy, the modern leadership is expected to develop people as the critical, and intellectual capital and asset of the enterprise.

Manager faces a variety of interesting and challenging situations and management process serves as a vital tool to assist him to achieve his objectives. However for effective management, managers require technical, interpersonal, conceptual, diagnostic skill to carry out his basic roles. Management skills may be acquired through education, training or experience and often combination of these depending upon the development of the necessary skills needed. Peter Drucker, the father of modern management, argues that organizational failures are ultimately a result of managerial failure. Therefore, to embrace change and to use it as a force, managers must transform themselves into leaders. Such leaders must maintain the willing support of their followers in providing products and services that meet the dynamic needs of a global economic vista, without looking backward.

BIBLIOGRAPHY

1. Bass, Bernard M.-'Stoghhill's Handbook of Leadership'/ Riverside N.J.: Free Press, 1981.
2. Daft, Richard.-'Organization Theory'/Minn.: St Paul West, 1986.
3. Katz, Robert L.-*The Skills of Effective Administrator*/ Haward Business Review, Sept.- Oct. 1974, pp 90-102.
4. Dr Khan, Wazir Ali, 'Applied Management for Engineers and technologists' ISBN 0-9526436-2-6
5. Dr Khan, Wazir Ali, 'Professional Manual on Total Quality Management' - ISBN 0-9526436-1-8
6. Dr Khan, Wazir Ali, 'Professional Manual on Total Project Management (Volume 1: CM General Perspective)'- ISBN 0-9526436-3-4
7. Dr Khan, Wazir Ali, 'Professional Manual on Total Project Management' (Volume 2: CM Commercial Perspective)'- ISBN 0-9526436-4-2
8. Dr Khan, Wazir Ali, 'Professional Manual on Claims Management and Dispute Resolution in Construction Process' - 0-9526436-7-7
9. Dr Khan, Wazir Ali, 'Fundamentals of Human Resources Development (First Edition)' - ISBN 0-9526436-0-X
10. Miner, John B.-'Theory of Organizational Structure and Process'/ Chicago: Dryden, 1982.
11. Newman, William H.-'Constructive Control'/ Englewood Cliffs, N.J.: Prentice-Hall, 1975.
12. Scott, William G. and David K. Hart.-'Organizational America'/ Boston: Houghton Miffin, 1979.

13. Steiner, George.-'Top Management Planning'/ New York: MacMillam, 1969.
14. Taylor, Fredrick W.-'Shop Management'/ New York: Harper & Row, 1903.
15. Weick, Karl E.-'*Amendment to Organizational Theorizing*'/ Academy of Management Journal, Sept. 1974, pp 487-502.
16. Whitely, William.-'Managerial Work Behavior: an Integration of results from two Major Approaches'/ Academy of Management Journal, June, 1985.